# The
# Thirlmere Way

## – a long-distance path from Manchester to The Lake District

## Tim Cappelli

**Published by Sigma Leisure** – an imprint of Sigma Press, 1 South Oak Lane, Wilmslow, Cheshire SK9 6AR, England.

Whilst every effort has been made to ensure that the information given in this book is correct, neither the publisher nor the author accept any responsibility for any inaccuracy.

**Printed and bound by**
Manchester Free Press, Paragon Mill, Jersey St., Manchester M4 6FP.

**British Library Cataloguing in Publication Data**
A CIP record for this book is available from the British Library.


ISBN: 1-85058-288-2

# PREFACE

The idea for this walk came to me several years ago whilst walking in the Lake District near Ambleside. Actually, I tell a lie. It never came to me at all, but was suggested to me by someone else. I was working, at the time, as a walking leader for a holiday company in the Lake District.

I would often take the group of guests up to High Sweden Bridge, behind Ambleside, as an introductory walk and on the way stop at a convenient black gate to point out and name the surrounding fells. It was some time before I discovered that this black gate was actually one of many hundreds of identical black gates which marked the route of the Thirlmere Aqueduct. When the Thirlmere valley was flooded in the 1890's to provide water for the thirsty population of Manchester, the engineers had to, some how, get the water from the Lake District to Manchester, over 90 miles away.

Their solution was simple. To dig an aqueduct out of the rock which would carry the water from Thirlmere at a height of 590 ft. above sea level, to the reservoirs in Manchester at a height of 360 ft. The difference in height would make the water run downhill all the way to Manchester. So this is what they did. What may be simple in theory, however, may not always be so in practice and the building of the Aqueduct took seven years to complete and the lives of many men. The tunnel blasted through Dunmail Raise alone, took over four years to complete, and is just one of several tunnels on the 95 mile length.

With a fall of just 20 inches to the mile, the water runs rather slowly down to Manchester, at a speed of 2 - 3 m.p.h.. The legend goes that after the Mayor of Manchester, Alderman John Mark, had turned on the valves at Thirlmere at a grand opening ceremony in 1894, he got on his horse and rode back to Manchester to open the valves at the other end, only to find that the water had not yet reached its destination. This fable, unfortunately, turns out to be just that, but this did not prevent me from repeating this story to my guests on the walk when showing, and explaining, to them the meaning of the black gates. I explained now the gates ran the whole length of the Aqueduct, so that a Water Authority Official could walk the whole length of the pipeline, from start to finish, in order to check the line for leaks or bursts. It was at this point that one of the guests suggested that this would make a good long distance walk and The Thirlmere Way was born.

The walk does not follow the route of the pipeline exactly since much of the line lies under private ground. Instead, I have tried to follow the Aqueduct as closely as possible using public footpaths, bridleways or tracks. This extends the walk from 95 miles to 137 miles, caused by the zig-zagging of the paths across the Aqueduct and the necessity to visit suitable resting places for the night

Each chapter in this book covers one days walking, there being ten chapters altogether and therefore ten days walking. It is, however, not compulsory to do the walk in ten days. On the contrary, I want you to enjoy this walk and if that means doing 30 miles a day and finishing after a few days, or doing a leisurely 8 miles a day and taking three weeks, that's fine. It's your walk! However, ten days seemed like a good choice and it means that each day ends at a small town or village where a bed can be found for the night. In each chapter I have included a map and route description for that days walking, as well as pointing out things of interest which you may see on the way. On a more practical side, I have included the address of somewhere to stay at the end of each chapter, or, in the case of the larger towns, directed you to the local Tourist Information Centre, whose kind and helpful staff will surely find you a bed for the night

Now, I realise that you might not be able to spare ten days off from work or might not wish to spend your two weeks holiday walking every day. For this reason I have also included an explanation on how to get to the start and finish of each section by both car and public transport. In this way you are free to do each days walk whenever you want, taking the car to the start and getting the bus back or taking the car to the finish and busing to the start or by using public transport to get there and back. You could even do the walk in reverse, going from the Lake District to Manchester, or walk the sections in any order you like. Flexibility, that's the thing and I have tried to cover every alternative for you. In addition, by using the maps and route descriptions in the book you should be able to walk the whole 137 miles without a map, though I'm sure you would feel better if you had the appropriate O.S. Landranger map. I know I would feel better if you did, and I'm sure you would get more out of the walk, and so I have listed the relevant map(s) at the start of each chapter. So you see, this book offers you a complete package - accommodation, transport, route descriptions and points of interest. The only thing I can't arrange is the weather, but then that's part of the fun of walking, isn't it. Isn't it?

It is at this point that I should say thank you to all those people without whom etc.. First of all a big thank you to North West Water, particularly Brian Ashworth, Mike Farrington and Paul Duff, who not only let me take up their valuable time with this crazy idea, but also let me copy out the route of the Thirlmere Aqueduct from their own maps, thereby risking national security. I would also like to thank Lancashire County Council for following up my comments on various public rights of way and to Terri Roberts who helped me with the complicated task of typing up my manuscript. A big thank you to my wife, Andrea, who supported me on the walk and encouraged me endlessly and finally to that anonymous guest who suggested the walk in the first place.

*Tim Cappelli*

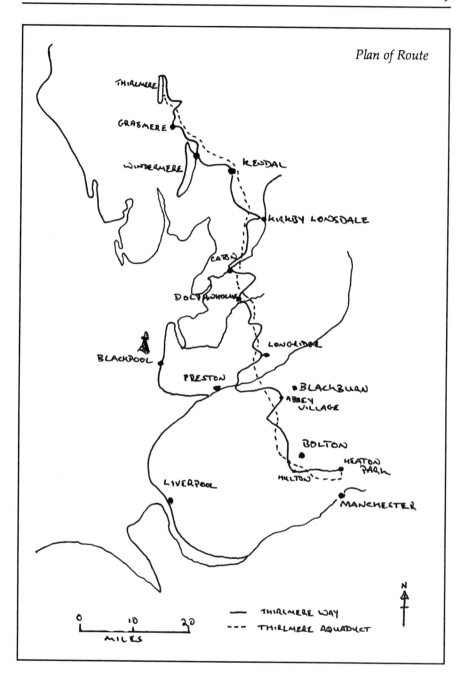

Plan of Route

THIRLMERE
GRASMERE
WINDERMERE
KENDAL
KIRKBY LONSDALE
CATON
DOLPHINHOLME
LONGRIDGE
BLACKPOOL
PRESTON
BLACKBURN
ABBEY VILLAGE
BOLTON
HEATON PARK
LIVERPOOL
HULTON
MANCHESTER

N

0        10        20
MILES

——— THIRLMERE WAY
- - - THIRLMERE AQUADUCT

# CONTENTS

# INTRODUCTION

## Thirlmere

"It appears on full consideration, that Thirlmere deserves your special attention as an independent source of supply to Manchester and I therefore recommend its adoption."

With these few words in a letter from John Fredric Bateman, the chief engineer to Manchester Corporation, to the council chairman in 1876, Thirlmere was chosen as the source of Manchester's drinking water. As the population and industry of Manchester increased in the 19th century, the demand on local water supplies became greater and greater, especially for clean, safe drinking water. The medical officer of Manchester at the time, Dr. Talham, once said, "If you supply me with an unlimited supply of good and pure water, I will be responsible for the health of the city.".

With this in mind Manchester set out to find that 'unlimited supply'. A few years earlier, the corporation had built a chain of seven reservoirs in the Longdendale Valley in the Derbyshire Peaks. This was now inadequate for the demands of the city and so Manchester looked at the Lake District to supply their needs. Why the Lake District, you ask? Why not build extra reservoirs in the Pennines nearer to Manchester? There were many reasons why not. First of all the Lake District, with the highest rainfall in the Country, offered a more reliable and larger supply than the Pennines ever could. The rural and sparsely populated Lake District would always have more water than it needed and also provide unpolluted water, due to the almost total lack of industry or human activity. Manchester also recognised the growing demand for water from other large towns in Lancashire, such as Preston and Burnley, and decided to leave the Pennines for more local use.

Manchester looked at both Ullswater and Haweswater before selecting Thirlmere. Thirlmere was chosen because it received more rainfall than the other two and because it was that much higher, something which was vital for their gravitational aqueduct to work. So, in 1877 Manchester applied for special powers from Parliament to use Thirlmere as a major reservoir and to construct the 95 mile aqueduct across Westmorland and Lancashire. This would involve building a 58ft high dam at the end of Thirlmere valley and raising the water by around the same height. At that time Thirlmere consisted of two small, narrow lakes called Leatheswater and Wythburn water.

As you can imagine, this proposal was not without its opposition, not least from the residents of Ambroth and Wythburn which were to be flooded by the scheme. The opposition rallied together to form The Thirlmere Defence Association, led by John Harwood a local landowner from Grasmere. They fought against Manchester on all fronts. People wrote letters to the national newspapers calling the act 'a piece of vandalism' and 'the destruction of a paradise'. They published a poem called 'The New Paradise Lost' to raise public support. They produced a colour map of the lake showing a vast expanse of oozy mud and rotting vegetation which, they claimed, would be exposed around the shores during the summer. They even produced a sample of this mud at an inquest on the matter to prove its smelliness.

Despite all this opposition and outrage, Manchester still managed to get the Thirlmere Bill passed in 1879 by a mixture of muscle and coercion. They quelled many local farmers by pointing out that, when the navvies came to build the dam and aqueduct, they could sell a lot more of their produce at far higher prices. They also promised to plant new forests around the lake to stop land erosion and prevent the oozy mud, as well as building two new roads around the lake. They claimed that by building a dam and raising the level of the lake, they were simply replacing a rock embankment that had been eroded away by the lake which was once much bigger anyway. In this way, they claimed, they were restoring the lake to its 'ancient condition'. In addition to this they offered the, soon to be flooded, landowners much more money for property than it was actually worth. However, most of the land in Thirlmere was owned by Thomas Leathe, Lord of the Manor of Legburthwaite, who was so against the idea that he refused the waterworks access to his land and even denied them permission to look at the lake, let alone sell the land.

After all, the land had been in the family for 300 years and the main lake was named after them. Nevertheless, surveys of the land went on in secret, and when Mr Leathes died in 1876 his son, who lived in Australia, was persuaded to sell the land. In all, Manchester bought 11,000 acres of land, covering the whole drainage area of Thirlmere from the crown of the mountains to the valley bottom and the chairman of the Water Committee, Alderman John Grave, was made Lord of the Manor of Legburthwaite.

Although the act was passed in 1879, work did not actually start on the dam and aqueduct until 1886, by which time the chairman of the committee had passed to Sir John Harwood who laid the foundation stone in the dam in August 1890. At the same time work on the 95 mile aqueduct started in earnest. In 1881 Manchester had laid out the entire route of the aqueduct with a long chain, in order to give landowners plenty of notice.

The idea behind the aqueduct was to follow the 500ft contour level as closely as possible, with a steady drop down to Manchester causing the water to run down-hill, by gravity, all the way. This would prove a difficult enough task by any standards, but when you consider the technology available to the Victorian engineers and the fact that this massive aqueduct was around 7ft in diameter, the whole feat seems incredible. Look at the room you are sat in. How large is it? 8ft, maybe 10ft wide? Now imagine digging a tunnel or trench as large as that all the way from Thirlmere to Manchester, and at the same time making sure it runs slightly down-hill all the way. Quite a feat!

The aqueduct starts with a 500 yard tunnel under Dunmail Raise. There are two other large tunnels under Nab Scar and Moor How and several shorter tunnels. Most of the remaining aqueduct consists of cut and cover tunnels, which involved digging out an 8ft wide trench, lining it with concrete and popping a concrete roof on top, before covering it up again. Where this was not possible the water was carried in four large cast-iron pipes. In this way the whole aqueduct has been hidden and, over the years, the countryside has returned to its original state. In fact the only clue to the lines existence are the visible pipelines, where the line crosses large rivers, and the black gates which mark the route. Ah yes, those famous black gates.

Time and time again you will spot these gates as you cross, and recross, the aqueduct on your way to its source. When you stand next to one of the gates as the line passes beneath a hedge or wall, you will be stood directly over the aqueduct, with several thousand gallons of water rushing under you feet. I decided to make a little competition of spotting the gates when I did the walk, seeing how many I could count on the 137 mile route. I managed to find 60 altogether and if you can beat this, I would certainly like to know. The rules are;- no binoculars and no leaving the route to find extra gates. The prize? Well, just the satisfaction of beating the author at his own game (which probably isn't very difficult). Just so you know what you are looking for, I've included a photograph of one in this introduction. By the way, they don't always come in pairs - a big clue!

The last piece of the aqueduct was put into place in August 1893 and the lake and aqueduct were officially opened in October 1894. The Prince of Wales was asked to perform the opening ceremony, but he was otherwise engaged. The task fell instead to Sir John Harwood, the Water Committee Chairman. On October 12th a grand procession of Aldermen and other dignitaries, were cheered through Ambleside and Grasmere on their way to Thirlmere. After several speeches by the mayor and others, Sir Harwood turned the wheels opening the valves, allowing the water to flow into the aqueduct for the first time. The next day, after the party had travelled back to Manchester by train (no fast horses, I'm afraid) a similar ceremony was held in Albert Square in Manchester.

For this special occasion the corporation had a temporary fountain built in the middle of the square, supplied directly by the Thirlmere Aqueduct. A dense crowd packed the square, many of them with drinking cups at the ready, waiting to be the first to try the sweet water of the Lakes. After several more speeches and the ringing of the town hall bells, Sir Harwood took out his special golden key and turned on the valves. The crowd cheered as the water sprayed out and Manchester got its first taste of Lakeland water.

Lake Thirlmere now held nearly 9,000 million gallons of water and could supply Manchester with 50 million gallons per day. The total cost of the scheme was around £1.5 million (such a project today would cost over £100 million) and had taken seven years to complete. When the idea of taking water from Thirlmere to Manchester was first proposed, one Lakeland local was heard to say "Theear's nut munny aneuf in aw t'world as wad deuh't". Fortunately for the people of Manchester, there was.

# The Walk

After the idea for the Thirlmere Way was born (or suggested!) I nurtured it carefully until a time arose when I could give it more attention. When that time came, I sat down with the relevant maps and thought that all I needed to do was join together a series of footpaths and bridleways and link them together by quiet lanes, just as Wainwright suggests in his Coast to Coast walk. This, in itself, was not a problem. However, I had set myself several conditions beforehand, which often proved difficult to achieve.

Firstly, I wanted to follow the route of the Aqueduct as closely as possible. After all, if the Thirlmere Way had any point, it had to cross the same countryside the Victorian engineers had to contend with 100 years ago. (This also scored the highest number of black gates!). However, I have not sacrificed all to the sacred aqueduct and have often chosen paths some miles from the pipeline in order to make the walk more enjoyable. For instance, on Day 5, between Dolphinholme and Caton, I have taken the walk over the edge of the Forest of Bowland. Though the pipeline contours around the hill some 1,000ft below, I think the excursion over Grit Fell to admire the view is worth it.

I also wanted to make sure that the walk followed only public rights of way or crossed areas of open access. There could then be no problem of future walkers being turned back or, even worse, prosecuted for trespassing. Most of the walk, then, is on public rights of way linked by quiet country lanes (though I have tried to keep tarmac pounding to a minimum). The only place I used access area paths was on Grit Fell on Day 5. Here Lancashire County Council have managed to negotiate access for walkers from the landowners, who use the fells for shooting. This means that this area is occasionally closed for shooting and I have included the 'phone number of the ranger responsible for this area who can tell you which days the area will be closed. (Most of the year you are safe!)

My last condition was one of accommodation.

Being a creature of comfort who needs a good night's rest, especially when walking, I decided that the walk would stop each day at a small town or village where such accommodation could be found. Unlike Wainwright I had no wish to avoid the tourist towns and instead made a bee-line for such places as Kendal (the largest town on the walk), Windermere and Grasmere. Here I knew a bed could be easily found. Kirkby Lonsdale was only second choice (sorry Kirkby Lonsdale - no offence) when I could only find a camp site at Hutton Roof. At all the other stopping off points, accommodation can be found, but it is often a case of Hobson's choice and so booking before hand would be advisable. Even this did not prove too much of a problem, except on Day 2.

Here I wanted to find somewhere to stay in the string of villages along the Leeds and Liverpool canal but found this quite impossible. Instead, I was pushed further and further towards Blackburn until I managed to find a bed near Abbey Village. This is why Day 2 is the longest day at 18.5 miles and deviates some way from the Aqueduct.

So, slowly, the walk evolved with minor changes en route until, finally, the Thirlmere Way was complete. I am not such a stickler for accuracy that you have to follow my route exactly, though. If you find a better path, or wish to visit somewhere off route, then fine. Go ahead. This is a description of my walk for you to follow if you wish or adapt to your needs. Just one last point. For security reasons, I am not allowed to show the route of the Aqueduct itself in any detail. So, I have not included the Aqueduct on any of the detailed maps in each chapter but only on the initial less detailed map. However, by spotting the black gates and referring to your O.S. maps, you could probably work out the exact route if you wanted to. One thing I would ask you. Don't go blowing the thing up, will you? It's probably against the Country Code.

*One of those black gates!*

# DAY 1: HEATON PARK TO HULTON

**Route:** Heaton Park – Clifton Junction – Walkden – Little Hulton – Over Hulton.

**Distance:** 14 miles

**Maps:** O.S. Landranger 1:50,000 No.109 Manchester and surrounding area.

**Getting There:** Heaton Park lies in the triangle formed by the A665, the A6044 and the A576. The easiest way into the park by car is on the A576. Coming from Manchester, the entrance for the park is the only left turn on the dual carriageway, just before the start of the M66. From the North, after leaving the end of the M66 and following the signs for Manchester, the entrance is the first turning on the right on the dual carriageway. This will take you to the car park next to Heaton House; the starting point.

The easiest way to get there by public transport is on the new Metrolink tramline from Manchester to Bury. Get off at Heaton Park station and the park entrance is directly opposite.

**Accommodation:** *Manchester* – There are many hotels in Manchester centre, from where you can easily catch the Metrolink. The Tourist Information Centre is based in the Town Hall in Lloyd Street. Tel. 061 234 3157.

*Hulton* – In this area I could only manage to find the one place to stay, the Mercury Hotel. This is a businessman's hotel where the rooms are quite expensive during the week but where the weekend rates are much cheaper.

Mercury Hotel, Manchester Road, Westhoughton, Gt. Manchester Tel. (0942) 813270.

# The Walk

Walking from the heart of Manchester's commuter belt and heading north-westwards to the edge of Bolton, one might expect to be walking through housing estates or industrial sites. However, this is not the case and although one or two places along the way would come under these headings, the vast majority of the walk today threads its way through the hidden greenery of Manchester. There are many things to stop and admire on the way, including the rarest flowers on the entire walk.

## Section 1. Heaton Park to Clifton Country Park

From the station, cross the road into the park entrance and follow the lane straight ahead. At the bottom of the hill and the T-junction of lanes, turn left and follow the wide lane for $1/4$ mile, past the small zoo on the left hand side. At the junction of lanes by the wooden benches turn right, then first left into the gardens of Heaton House. In front of the house is a large fountain. (If you arrived by car, the house and fountain can be found next to the car park.)

This is the start of the walk. The fountain was taken from Albert Square in Manchester. Since the first water from Thirlmere arrived at a similar fountain in Albert Square, This is a good place to start the walk. The actual reservoir where the Aqueduct finishes is in the north of the park, but is closed to the public and there is not much to see. The Aqueduct runs south from the reservoir, under the park, then turns west about 1 mile south of our walk.

To start the Thirlmere Way, retrace your steps through the park to the station. (Follow the instructions above in reverse if you are a car user).

Heaton Hall was built in 1772 by James Wyatt for the Earl of Wilton, Sir Thomas Egerton, and is said to be the best 18th Century house in Manchester. The house and estate of 638 acres was given to Manchester to use as a park in 1902. As you walk back to the station notice the grand arch towering over the trees. This was once part of the Grecian façade of Manchester's original Town Hall. When this was pulled down to make the new Town Hall in Albert Square a piece of the facade was saved and put up here, in Heaton Park.

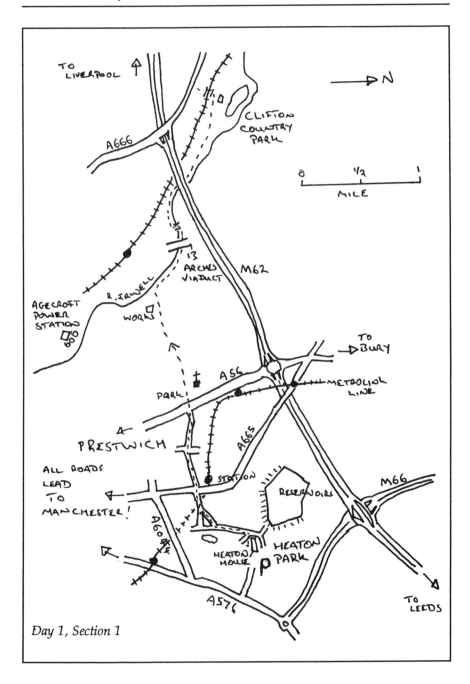

Day 1, Section 1

*Heaton Hall and the Start of the Walk.*

At the park entrance take the road on the left of the station (Whittaker Lane) and follow this road until it becomes Rectory Lane at the crossroads. Carry straight on down Rectory Lane, following the road as it bends to the left (now St. Mary's Road) to the T-junction with the main A56 (Bury New Road).

> This is part of Prestwich, now a busy commuter town of Manchester. In 1795, when J. Arkin wrote 'A description of the country around Manchester', Prestwich was a small country parish with, Arkin claimed, "pure and falubrious *(sic)* air." To prove his point he listed the parish's eight oldest residents from the Doctor at 70, to the sexton's wife, Mary Berry at 86. The air of Prestwich today is anything but falubrious!

Cross the A56 and into the park opposite. Cross the formal gardens and head right towards the church. Go through the V-gateway on the right and then take the path to the left, away from the church. Follow this path which leads down to some steps down to a footbridge. Go down the steps but do not cross the bridge. Instead follow the path by the stream, keeping the stream on your left. Continue on the path, past another footbridge and on to the next, smaller footbridge. Cross this bridge and then turn right following the path with the stream now on your right.

> The woods here are a pleasant mixture of horse chestnut and oak with plenty of water-loving plants such as iris and Himalayan balsam. The balsam is easy to spot, with its large leaves and pink flowers like little helmets. If you are doing this walk in Autumn, try touching the seed pods and you will find out why it is also called touch-me-not balsam!

Where the path joins another, by a stone bridge, bear left on the main path and follow this to a wooden 5-bar gate. Go through the gate to the tarmac road on the right.

> Notice the cooling towers of Agecroft power station on your left. Powered by coal from Agecroft Colliery, this is where the Aqueduct crosses the River Irwell in large cast-iron pipes supported by an ornate iron bridge.

Turn left on the road and walk down to the bottom, following the public footpath sign. After 300 yards take the path on the right through the metal gate. Follow the path across the field, bearing left where the path meets another track. This track leads down past the large pylon and by the river. At the river turn right to follow the wide track towards the 13 arches viaduct in the distance.

> You are now on part of the Irwell Valley Way, a long distance walk from Manchester to the source of the Irwell in Rossendale. The 13 arch bridge is a listed viaduct built in 1846 to carry the Clifton Junction to Rawtenstall branch of the East Lancashire Railway over the Irwell Valley. You can just about count all the arches from here.

Walk underneath the 13 arches viaduct and then turn left over the disused canal bridge. After crossing the bridge turn right and follow the path between the factory and the river.

If you come this way between April and July, you will probably spot the great number of purple orchids along this path, the only orchids on the entire walk. All plants have a name, of course, but how do they get that name? Some, like buttercup, are obvious. Others are not so clear. Orchid? Well the orchid gets its name from the shape of its roots which consists of two small spheres covered in hairs, and orchis is Latin for a certain part of the male body!

*13 Arches Bridges, Near Prestwich.*

Continue on the path by the river, under the M62, over the stile and follow the right hand fork by the river. Cross the wooden footbridge and onto the track. Here turn right and continue to a junction of tracks and then turn left to follow the track under the power lines.

Notice the information board here which tells how this area was once Clifton Colliery, the first deep shaft mine in the area. The coal was transported by canal barge, loaded at nearby Clifton Marina, to the Manchester, Bolton and Bury canal. The colliery is now being restored and the area being turned into a Country Park by Manchester Archeological Unit and Salford Council.

Continue on this track to the car park and visitor's centre.

## Section 2. Clifton Country Park to Little Hulton

At the car park turn left, through the entrance and then left again under the railway bridge and onto the housing estate. Turn left on the road and follow the road uphill to where the road meets the main road (A666). Cross the road and turn right. After 20 yards take the path on the left behind the housing estate. Go straight ahead on this path as it leads through a gap in the fence, behind the houses and into the field. Cross this and the next field following the fence on the right hand side. At the second stile turn right over another stile and follow the path by the barbed-wire fence. Over two more stiles and onto a clearer path by the engraved stone telling when Clifton Moss was first cultivated. Continue on this path, over two more stiles, to a clearing which looks, at first sight, like a golf fairway. Here turn left and head towards the motorway, passing between the pylon and the house to the path by the motorway. Follow this path to the footbridge and cross the motorway.

This bridge, built to keep open a public right of way when the motorway was built, is fairly impressive to cross. Crossing 10 lanes of traffic, the noise and roar may not be appealing to a walker but it's definitely a sight to see. You can stand on the bridge and gloat a little at the poor people below, whizzing northwards in their little boxes to the Lake District. You're taking the scenic route.

On the other side of the M61, follow the path straight ahead, past the bungalow and then round to the right until you pass the farm buildings and garden centre. Here the track bends to the left, but ignore this and instead carry straight on towards the large white cylinders in the distance. The path becomes a wide track along a disused railway line, passing the white cylinders on the left and then straight across another

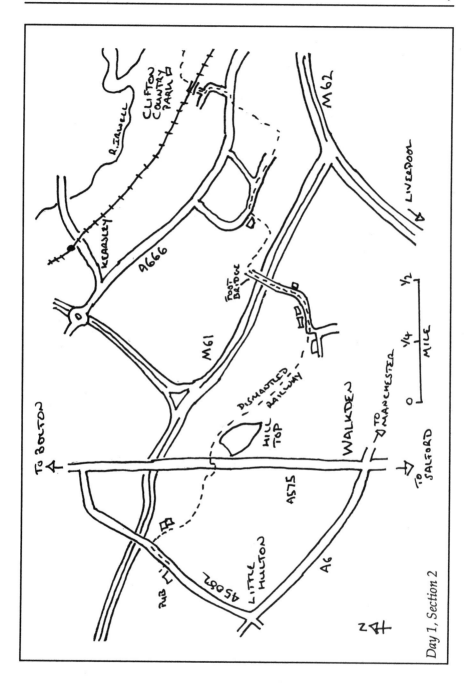

Day 1, Section 2

track. Continue straight ahead to pass Hill Top reservoirs on the left after another $1/2$ mile and follow the path up to the road on the right.

The whole area of Hill Top which you have just passed through, at present derelict and neglected, is soon to be turned into a landscaped nature area by Salford Groundwork Trust. They plan to plant woodlands, build picnic sites and bird hides and install play areas for the children. The Aqueduct, by the way, is now closer than at any time since leaving Heaton Park and lies just the other side of Hill Top reservoir.

On the road turn left to the main road (A575). Cross the road, turn left and then right after 20 yards down Grosvener Road. Take the steep path on the right, back down to the disused railway line. Follow this as it leads onto a wider track. Here turn right and follow the main track past the slag heaps and towards the large warehouses, then follow it left, past the industrial units on the right hand side, to the main road (A5802).

This is probably the least attractive part of the whole walk, but fortunately does not last too long. The Aqueduct is about $1/2$ mile to the south and just at this point, it splits. The main part heads east towards Heaton Park, whilst a branch heads south, around Manchester, to form the rings mains. This is a large circular pipeline, completely surrounding and supplying Manchester.

## Section 3. Little Hulton to Over Hulton

At the road turn left and walk along the road for $1/4$ mile to the Dukes Gate pub. Just before the pub turn right and follow the path which leads across the piece of waste ground, passing the housing estate on the left hand side. Follow the paths heading right towards the power lines until you reach the side of the motorway. Continue on the path by the motorway, which runs between the motorway and the houses and onto the road bridge over the motorway. Turn left on this road, following it round to the right then on 300 yards to Moorhey Road on the right. Turn down this road to find the path on the right between houses 29 and 27. Turn down this path, cross the golf fairway to the footbridge over the M61. Do not cross the bridge but turn left and walk along the side of the fairway and then, just before the pylon, along the path leading off through the rough. This roughly follows the motorway to a stile. (The original right of way here lies between the two wooden fences on your right, but is much too overgrown to use.) Go over the stile and continue on the path through the scrub, past the subway, then on until the path bends sharply left and leads to the main road (A6). Turn right along the road and follow it to the roundabout. Cross the roundabout and follow the A6 for another 30 yards to the farm track on the left (Back Lane). Turn left and follow this track.

> Notice your first two black gates. This is the first time since Heaton Park that you have recrossed the Aqueduct. As these are your first two black gates, I have told you where they are – but no more clues!

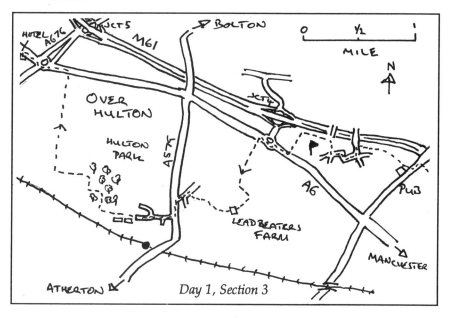

Day 1, Section 3

Follow the track for $^1/_2$ mile then take the first lane to the right to Leadbeaters Farm. Walk into the farmyard (the first of many with a barking dog on a chain) and turn right up the track which leads through a wooden 5-bar gate and on to meet another track going left to right. Turn left on this track and follow it until it passes the white house and onto the road. Follow the road down to the left (Breeze Hill Road), across Lansdowne Road and straight ahead to the main road (A579). Turn left and follow the road for 300 yards to Broadway on the right.

Turn right down Broadway and where the road forks, take the left fork to the fields behind the houses.

Notice the small stone plaque in the field on the right of the gate. This is a memorial to the 344 men and boys who died in a pit disaster here in 1910. The stone is now used by the cows as a scratching post.

On the left of the gate is a small path running behind the houses. Follow this path which leads behind the housing estate and, after $1/4$ mile, to a bus stop on the road. Here turn right and follow the path into the woods.

These are Hulton Park woods and although the park is a private estate, the locals have access to the woods and there is a public right of way through here. The locals use it for walking, bike riding and fishing and, as a result, the woods are a mass of paths where it is all too easy to get lost. In fact, we did just that, just as my wife reached her low point on the walk. It was she who christened these woods 'Hell Woods', so follow these directions carefully!

Follow the path until a junction of several paths is reached. Go straight ahead on the path slightly to the right up the steep embankment. Cross the next path going left to right and straight ahead to the next junction of paths at the pond. Here turn left and follow the main path through the woods, ignoring all paths off to the left and right, to the stile at the edge of the woods. Over this and then the next stile to follow the path across the field. Over the next stile and onto the track. Follow this track, which becomes a clear farm track, and on 200 yards to the stile on the right. Go over this stile and follow the path for 1 mile to the main road (A6). On the road turn left and follow it to the large roundabout and shops. Go straight ahead at the roundabout, following the A6, and the hotel is 200 yards on, on the left.

# DAY 2: HULTON TO ABBEY VILLAGE

**Route:** Hulton-Chewmoor-Lostock-Rivington-Wheelton-Abbey Village.

**Distance:** 18¹/₂ miles

**Maps:** O.S. Landranger 1:50,000 No.109 Manchester and surrounding area O.S. Landranger 1:50,000 No.102 Preston and Blackpool

**Getting There:** The start of the walk is at Chequerbent – the roundabout where the A6 meets the A676. By car then, follow the A6 from either Preston or Manchester or the A676 from Bolton or Westhoughton, until this large roundabout is reached. If coming any distance, the roundabout is ¹/₂ mile from Junction 5 of the M61. Head for Westhoughton when you come off the motorway and Chequerbent is the first roundabout. The Mercury Hotel is 200 yards from the roundabout, heading north on the A6. There are many buses from either Manchester or Bolton, travelling to Chorley that will take you to Chequerbent. For example, the 37, 38 and 129 from Manchester or the 127, 401 and 500 from Bolton. The nearest train station is Lostock on the Bolton to Preston Line. This is about 1¹/₂ miles into the walk and starting from here cuts out much of the road walking. For Abbey Village see chapter 3.

**Accommodation:** Day 2 caused me the biggest problem, accommodation wise, and though I wanted to find somewhere to stay in the Wheelton area, I found this impossible. Instead the walk had to be diverted slightly to Abbey Village. Here I found not one, but two places for a weary traveller:

Karenza Guest House, Bolton Road, Withnell, Lancs. (0254 830070).

The Royal, Bolton Road, Abbey Village, Lancs. (0254 830206).

# The Walk

The longest day. I have to admit, the day does not start off with much promise, with nearly a mile of road walking, then across a golf course, derelict sites and old peat cuttings. Please, stick with it though. Once past the first few miles, you cross the border into Lancashire and the walk improves dramatically. Through Lever Park with its pleasant reservoirs and woods, over Healy Nab with magnificent views across the plains of Lancashire and then by the Leeds and Liverpool canal with its quietly chugging barges, today's walk offers variety and interest all the way.

# Section 1. Hulton to Horwich

From the hotel, walk along the A6 towards Preston for 400 yards to the footpath sign by the white house. The sign is of a little white man striding out. (Not only is this sign sexist, but the poor man has no provisions, waterproofs or even a woolly hat!). Turn right and follow the sign across the field to the road on the other side. Turn left, and at the end of the road turn right down Chewmoor Lane. Follow this road for $3/4$ mile to Chewmoor, passing under the M61 for the last time. Pass the Duke of Wellington pub and on another 200 yards to the sharp right-hand bend in the road. Here follow the public footpath sign to the left down Chulsey Gate Lane. Follow this lane for over $1/2$ mile as it leads to Moss Hall Farm. Walk through the farmyard and out on the track at the far end. Continue on the track which leads through the fields for $1/4$ mile as it bends first right then left towards the houses by the motorway. At the houses turn right on the tarmac track to pass in front of the buildings and on for another $1/4$ mile to the road. Turn right on the road and follow it for 150 yards to the sharp left bend. Here walk straight ahead on the farm track past the large house on the right. Continue down this track for $1/4$ mile to the house and farm at the end. Turn right into Gibralter Farm and then left between the house and the garage. Go over the stile here and walk down to the railway bridge.

Looking across to the left from here you can see frustrated golfers slicing their balls across Lostock Golf Course. In the middle of the golf course is the large underground balancing reservoir for the Thirlmere Aqueduct which was built to cope with fluctuating demands. In fact, the original plan of Manchester Corporation was to build the large terminal reservoirs, now at Heaton Park, here near Bolton. However, because of the smoke and pollution from Bolton's industry, the entire reservoir would had to have been underground. This would have been much too expensive and

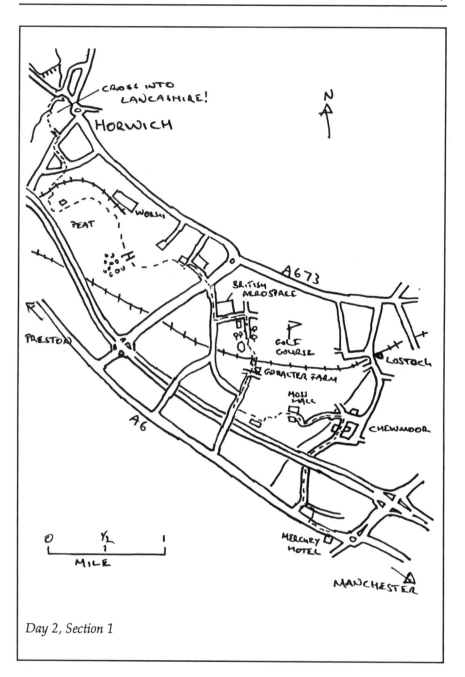

*Day 2, Section 1*

instead they extended the line to Prestwich where the air was falubrious! So, you can blame Victorian Bolton for having to walk the previous 16 miles. Otherwise you could have started here. There is also a large treatment works here at Lostock, built in 1988. One of the conditions of the Thirlmere Bill granted to Manchester in 1879, was that it had to use the water to supply towns along the route of the aqueduct. One such town is Bolton who were first charged 6d by Manchester, for every 1,000 gallons of water.

On the other side of the bridge go through the metal gate and continue straight ahead by the old hedge to a large, overgrown pond. On the right of the pond is a clear track through the trees. Follow this track as it leads behind a farm to a junction of tracks by some works. Here turn left on the track between the works on the right and the farm on the left. Turn right at the house with the peacocks to follow the lane by the side of the works and onto the road.

The works are actually British Aerospace's Dynamic Division. This doesn't describe the workforce, but what they produce. It is here that they develop and build missiles for use by the armed forces.

At the road, turn right and across the dual carriageway at the lights to walk up the road opposite. At the end of this road follow the track straight ahead to Sefton Fold Farm Garden Centre. Turn left into the garden centre and then follow the footpath signs which lead behind the farm, along an overgrown path and over a stile into a field. In the field bear slightly to the left and follow the faint path to a gap in the barbed wire fence on the opposite side of the field. Here, bear slightly left again towards an old hedge and then follow the hedge to a stile in the corner of the field. Go over the stile and straight across the next field to the wooden bridge over the ditch. Over this, across the next field and another bridge and turn right following the path to the dirt track. (This track is used by lorries taking their load to the landfill site on your left). Cross this track and follow another which leads straight ahead. Continue on this track as it runs along the bottom of an embankment on the right (ignoring other paths off to the left and right) and then bears left after $1/2$ mile towards the motorway in the distance.

Although the landscape here does not look very inviting, I did see my first dragonfly of the walk here, so keep your eyes open. I can't tell you which species the dragonfly was, but I can tell you that it was a hawker! There are two types of dragonfly – hawkers and chasers. Hawkers hover around, looking for something to feed on. When they see a juicy fly or insect, they pounce, diving on their prey from behind. Chasers, meanwhile, sit on a flower or blade of grass and wait for their prey to pass by. When it does, they dive out and give chase. The sharks of the insect world! Along this stretch you will also see piles of peat bricks drying in the sun, ready to be burnt on the fire. These bricks have been cut out of the ground here using an old peat-cutting machine. This old yellow engine was parked up by the side of the track when I came past, but if you are lucky, you may get to see it in action.

Follow this track for a further $1/4$ mile until you reach the farm. Go through the farmyard to the motorway and the stile on the right. Go over the stile and follow the path by the side of the motorway until you reach the railway. Turn right and follow the fence by the railway for 100 yards to the wooden footbridge on the left. Cross the bridge and pass under the railway, minding your head on the low bridge. On the other side, turn right and follow the path leading between the channelled stream and the railway embankment. Continue on this path behind the houses until you reach the end of a chain link fence. Turn left here, across the footbridge, and onto the road. Turn left on the road then take the first right and follow this road to the main road (B5238).

Turn right on the B5238 and then left after 100 yards down Edward Street. Follow the public footpath sign along the track to the stream. You are now in Lancashire and will be for the next 5 days and $64^1/2$ miles. Turn right and along the stream to the stone bridge. Cross the bridge onto the tarmac drive and turn right following the drive to the main road (A673).

## Section 2. Horwich to Healey Nab

At the road turn right and walk along the road for 200 yards to the first turning on the left (signed Rivington). Turn left up this lane and follow it for $1/4$ mile, past the sharp right bend to the bridleway on the left which runs between the concrete bollards.

On the way up this road, look over the wall on your left to see the filter beds of a large water treatment works. Ah, you think, another feature of the Thirlmere Aqueduct. I'm afraid not. This is one of the paradoxes of water supply. Whilst you are walking 137 miles to the source of Manchester's drinking water, here you are on the edge of Manchester, passing Rivington and Anglezarke reservoirs which supply water to Liverpool over 30 miles away! The large reservoirs which you will soon pass, were built in the 1860's by Liverpool Corporation when they too had the same problems as Manchester in finding water. In fact, when Manchester first started exploring the Lake District for a suitable supply, they did so in conjunction with Liverpool. The original idea was to use Ullswater and Haweswater to supply both cities in a joint scheme. However, Liverpool decided to opt out and instead concentrate on North Wales. This is one of the reasons Manchester turned its attention to Thirlmere.

Turn left and follow the bridleway which leads onto a path in the woods. You are now in Lever Park and there are toilets and a car park just off to the right here should you need them. Otherwise, follow the path straight ahead through the woods until you come to a wide track at a cross roads of paths. Turn left here and follow the wide track for 100 yards to a kissing gate on the left. Go through this and follow the path through the woods, over the footbridge, up the steps and, keeping the wooden fence on your left follow the path to the reservoir edge.

This whole area was once owned by the Pilkington family who lived at Rivington Hall until 1616. The land was then sold and eventually passed to Lord Leverhulme. A local boy made good, William Lever made his fortune with Sunlight soap and set up Lever Brothers, now a multi-million pound company. Lord Willie (as he was known to his friends) was a benevolent boss and built a 'model village' for his workers at Port Sunlight in Liverpool and in 1900 he gave the land here as a gift to the public. Before doing so he restored the two old barns of Rivington, believed to have been built before the Normans, and built a bungalow based on an Italian villa. It even had terraced gardens complete with grottos and waterfalls. All these buildings are still in Lever Park and are open to the public. One of the barns is now an information centre – but you won't see these today without a diversion, which you really have not got time for, so continue...

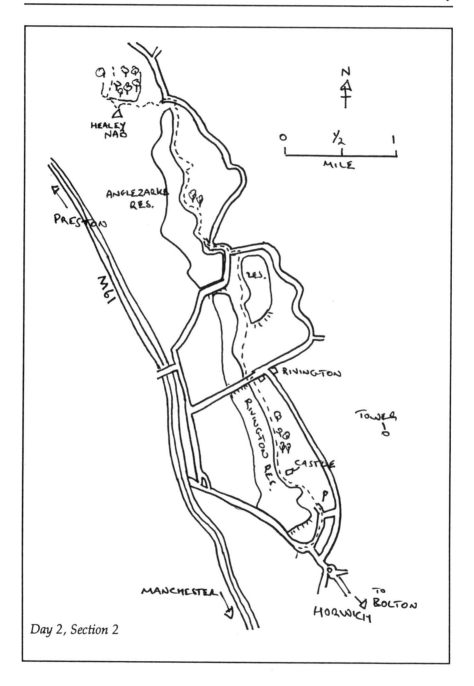

*Day 2, Section 2*

Follow the path by the reservoir until you reach the castle.

*Rivington Castle- a copy of a derelict castle.*

Ah, now here is something of Lord Lever which you can admire. He built this replica of Liverpool Castle here as a folly when he owned the land, though why anybody should want to build a replica of a derelict castle is beyond me. The tower you have probably seen up on the hill is not another of Lord Lever's follies, but was built by a Mr. Adams in 1724 to "provide rest and shelter for those whom curiosity urges to the fatigue and peril of the ascent". What a kind chap.

Go past the castle and straight ahead, following the path through the trees by the reservoir. After $1/4$ mile, when the main path bends to the right, take the path down to the left by the wooden fence and back to the lakeside. Follow this path for another $1/2$ mile until you reach a parking area which leads onto the road by the primary school.

This school, now Rivington Primary School, was originally Rivington Grammar School founded in 1568. Built by the Pilkington
family, the school was renowned for its high standards. Discipline
was strict and the original school rules included, 'no street bawls,
no haunting of ale houses and no brandishing daggers in school'.
The school is part of Rivington village, much of which was flooded
when the reservoirs where built. Liverpool was obliged to improve
and rebuild what was left of the village as part of the deal.

On the road turn left towards the dam, then right just after Rivington
Village Club. Follow the lane by the water for $1/4$ mile to a metal gate on
the left. Go through this gate and follow the lane on the other side for
$3/4$ mile to the road. Turn left to follow the road downhill to the
junction. Turn right at the junction and follow the road for 150 yards to
the signpost at the sharp bend. Go straight ahead (Signed Anglezarke car
park) and where the lane bends right and uphill take the branch on the
left through the kissing gate. Walk along this track for $1/2$ mile until it
becomes a road and starts to zig-zag uphill. On one of the zigs (or zags!)
is a wooden bench by an information board on local birdlife. Here take
the path between the bench and the board which leads into the woods.
Continue on this path for $1/2$ mile until it leads away from the water and
comes to a junction of paths. Turn left to follow a path which leads back
towards the reservoir. Follow this clear path until you reach the road.

Look out for the large clumps of Himalayan balsam as you reach
the road. If you missed it in Prestwich yesterday, here it is again.

On the road turn left, past the half-timbered house and across the dam
to the public footpath sign on the left. Go over the stile here and turn
right, up the steps to the ladder stile. Go over the stile and follow the
path by the fence on the right hand side, to the next stile. Over this and
across the bridleway to follow the path uphill, through the heath. This is
Healey Nab, our first piece of heathland, but certainly not our last.
Continue on this path which crosses a clear track and leads to the edge
of a wood on the right. At the wood, keep to the path with both the
wood and wall on your right and follow it uphill to the cairn on the
summit of Healey Nab.

## Section 3. Healey Nab to Abbey Village

At the top of Healey Nab, stop and take in the magnificent view which stretches out in front of you. Look across at Chorley and beyond to the sea with the infamous gasometers of Southport on the horizon. In the 14th Century Healey Nab was a Royal Forest. If you wanted to agistment your cattle (Summer and Winter them) or pannage your pigs (feed them on beech nuts and acorns) then you had to pay the King for the privilege. The land here became so rich in livestock at that time, that in 1322 the Scots raiders, who were just the other side of the Ribble, pushed south making a bee-line for the Nab. They drove away all the pannaging pigs and agistmenting cows. There were no revenues for the King that year!

From the summit cairn continue by the wall and woods, now walking downhill, until you reach a stile and then a meeting of paths on the edge of the woods. Turn immediately right after the stile to follow the bridleway through the woods. Continue on this bridleway, ignoring all paths off to the side, and out of the woods on the other side. Continue straight ahead to cross the fields on a path which becomes a dirt track and then past the houses to the road. Turn left and walk down the road to the T-junction. Go straight across the road and follow the public footpath sign by the metal gate. Follow this path (looking out for the Jays which can often be seen here) to pass under the railway bridge, then straight ahead through the gap in the trees. Keeping the hedge to your left, walk to the far corner of the field, over the stile and continue by the hedge to a track by a house. Follow the track to the road. On the road turn left and walk downhill to the junction with the main road (A674). Cross the main road and down the road opposite. Follow this road round to the right and on for 300 yards to Wheelton Village.

Wheelton was originally a much smaller village which, like so many other small towns in Lancashire, developed around a cotton mill. The mill has now gone, but the rows of mill-workers houses still remain. By the way I hope you didn't miss those black gates back there!

At the Red Lion Pub turn left down Blackburn Road, past the Post Office and along the tarmac path at the end to the road again. Carry on for another 300 yards to the path on the left, just before the houses. Turn left

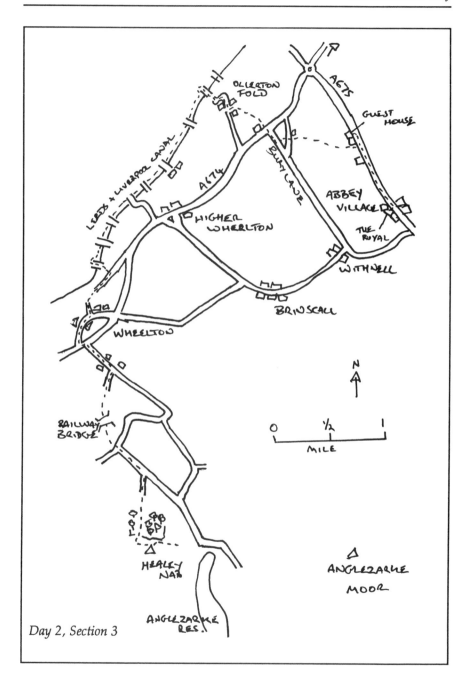

*Day 2, Section 3*

down this path which leads down to the Leeds and Liverpool canal. Cross the bridge, onto the tow-path and turn left to follow the canal towards Leeds. Walk along the tow-path for 2 miles to the seventh bridge after the one you have just crossed.

The Leeds and Liverpool canal. Now with only the odd, chugging barge or leisurely canoeist, it's difficult to think that this waterway was once the M62 of its time. Its designer, John Longbottom, worked for Yorkshire and submitted his plans in 1768. Liverpool felt that the plans needed checking by Brindley, the famous canal builder, and got him to look at the designs. Yorkshire, understandably, took this as a snub and refused to pay out any more money on the scheme until Liverpool had raised an equal amount. After many such fallings-out between Liverpool and Yorkshire, the first stretch was opened in 1773. It wasn't until 1817, however, that the whole 127 mile canal was completed. Not surprising considering the arguing that went on!

Now's your chance to relax. No navigation problems, just things to look out for on the way. For instance, see how many types of birds you can spot, from coots to kingfishers. Or take in the great variety of wild flowers along the tow-path. At the fourth bridge along, look over to the right and see if you can spot the great sandstone aqueduct with its six great arches. This actually carries the Thirlmere Aqueduct across the stream here and, if you've got the time, it's worth crossing this bridge to have a closer look. Look out for the square chimney of Withnell Fold paper mill, also on the right. Originally built in 1843, this mill once produced the paper for British banknotes. When you reach the seventh bridge, you will notice the next bridge a few hundred yards further up the canal. Between these two bridges is the point where the Thirlmere Aqueduct crosses the canal.

Just before the seventh bridge, go over the stile on the left and then cross the bridge to the other side of the canal. Go straight ahead up the fenced track and over the stile at the top. Cross the track, over the stile opposite and on into Ollerton Fold, a small collection of houses and farms. Walk straight on and just after Ollerton Farm Cottage go left over the stone stile (with a gate on top!) following the yellow arrow. Turn left and between the garage and house onto the mowed lawn. Here head right to the diagonally opposite corner of the field, and a stile. Over this and bear left to a wooden footbridge. After the footbridge turn right to the stile in the hedge and then straight ahead to pass the big white house on your right and onto the main road (A674). Cross this road and walk up the road opposite (Bury Lane) for 300 yards. At the end of the wooden fence on the left is a stile. Over the stile, cross the field, heading for the house opposite, and onto the lane. Cross the lane and walk down the track by the side of the house. Continue for 350 yards to a metal 5-bar gate. Go over the stile on the left of the gate and follow the hedge on your right to the ladder stile in the corner. Now go straight ahead, heading for the solitary tree. From the tree continue in a straight line to the clear gap in the hedge opposite. At the gap, follow the track straight ahead to the wooden 5-bar gate and the main road (A675). Here you have a choice. If you have booked into the Karenza Guest House, turn left and walk 100 yards to the guest house. If you have booked into The Royal Public House or are getting the bus home, then turn right and walk $1/2$ mile into Abbey Village. (The guest house has its obvious advantages!)

*Following the Leeds and Liverpool Canal.*

# DAY 3: ABBEY VILLAGE TO LONGRIDGE

**Route:** Abbey Village – Hoghton Bottoms – Samlesbury Bottoms – Roach Bridge – Brockhole Bridge – Longridge.

**Distance:** 14 miles.

**Map:** O.S. Landranger 1:50,000 No.102 Preston and Blackpool.

**Getting There:** Abbey Village is on the A675 from Bolton to Preston. Just follow this road from either direction until Abbey Village is reached. If coming from Blackburn or Chorley and the M61, follow the A674 until the roundabout with the A675 is reached. Here turn south (left from Blackburn, right from Chorley) along the A675 and Abbey Village is 2 miles on. There are several buses which run to Abbey Village from Bolton, Blackburn and Chorley. The nearest train station is again at Blackburn from where a bus can be caught. The buses are the 124 and the 259, Blackburn to Chorley (or vice versa). For Longridge see chapter 4.

**Accommodation:** At Longridge I managed to find a very nice bed and breakfast at Charnley House. This is an 18th century farmhouse with several rooms, including 'The Penthouse' on the top floor – a small self-contained flat where you can comfortably collapse after a hard day's walk. The rates here are very good and the hostess friendly.

Charnley House, Preston Road, Alston, Longridge, Lancs PR3 3BD. Tel. (0772) 782800.

The only other accommodation in Longridge is a caravan site to the northeast of the village. There are several pubs in the village itself but as far as I know none offer accommodation.

# The Walk

Today is a lovely day's walk with the promise of dippers, herons and other water birds to be glimpsed as you follow the route of two of Lancashire's major rivers. First along the Darwen as it flows, dirty and abused, from the industrial towns of Darwen and Blackburn, and then along the mighty Ribble, the main river of Lancashire, winding its way across the wide valley bottom. There is a great contrast in scenery too. The obvious riverside walks with hogweed and rushes in abundance; woodland walks through oak and sycamore; walks across pastures with lapwings calling out warnings as you pass their nests and walks through Victorian industrial villages built around paper and cotton mills some still in use and some long since gone. With so many things to see, we'd better get started!

## Section 1. Abbey Village to Hoghton Bottoms

Abbey Village gets its name from its connection with Whalley Abbey. There was once, according to legend, a secret passage from Brinscall Hall to the west, through this area, to Whalley Abbey. Why anybody should want such a long secret passage is unknown, though it was probably for the same purpose as all the priest holes and hiding places at nearby Samlesbury Hall – to hide the priests and monks during the reformation. During the industrial revolution Abbey Village built up around the large cotton mill here which provided jobs for the workers who lived in the terraced houses of the village. The mill closed in 1970.

From Abbey Village walk back up the A675 for 3/4 mile to the Karenza Guest House. From the guest house, cross the road and go over the stile by the gate. Cross the field to the track and turn left to follow the track for 1/4 mile. Here the track bears sharp right and on the left is a stile onto a parallel track. Go over this stile and turn right along this track to the farm. Walk past the farm buildings, turn left through the gate and follow the path across the field which leads downhill to the canal bridge at the bottom. Notice the tower on a hill off to your right. This is Darwen Tower, a famous local landmark built to commemorate the Diamond Jubilee of Queen Victoria in 1897. It also acts as a monument to

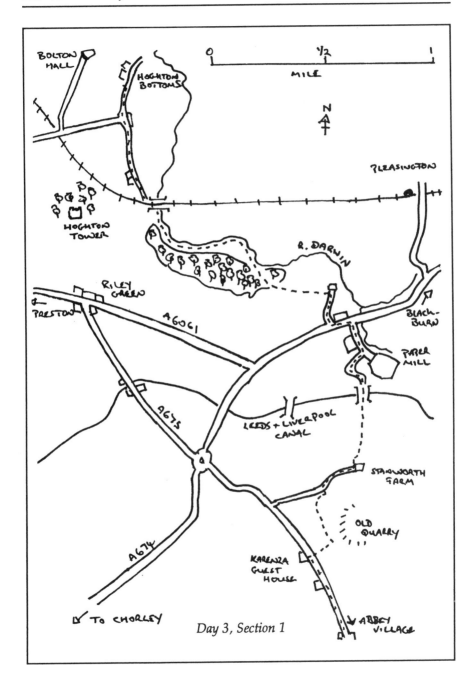

Day 3, Section 1

the small group of Darwen men who, in 1878, fought to keep the paths across the fell open to the public.

Go over the canal and follow the path on the other side which leads down to the paper mill. Here turn left along the river by the works to the main road (A674). At the road turn left and walk past the row of terraced houses, (originally built for workers in the mill and are probably still owned by mill workers), turn immediately right up the track by the houses for 200 yards to the metal gate on the left. Go through this gate, cross the field, over the stile and bear left through a gateway on the other side of the field and to the edge of the woods on the right. Here there is a stile into the woods. Go over this and follow the path downhill through the woods to the river. Follow the path by the river which leads through woods, clearings and more woods for nearly 1 mile until a railway bridge with its enormous arch is reached.

It is along this stretch that I spotted both a heron and a dipper on the river as well as several squirrels running along the branches of trees. The heron was easy to spot, with its lazy flight, long, wide wings and long legs stuck out behind. The dipper isn't as easy. This small, dark brown bird with a white front is easiest to spot as it sits on rocks in the river looking for small fish to dive at. The river Darwen may not be the cleanest river in the world, but its certainly not the dirtiest and has improved greatly in the last few years, evidence of which is the sight of the dipper bobbing up and down on the rocks.

Amongst the many plants you will see, one of the largest will certainly be the butterbur. It has enormous green leaves with a large spike of purple flowers growing from the middle of the plant. Often found by rivers and wet places, the large leaves of the butterbur were once used to wrap freshly made butter in, either to keep it cool or to carry it to market. It's not hard to see how the plant got its name!

Walk under the railway bridge and onto the road. Follow this road for $1/2$ mile to the road junction. Here follow the road right and downhill (Valley Road) for 200 yards to a group of buildings on the left. This is Hoghton Bottoms.

## Section 2. Hoghton Bottoms to Brockhole Bridge

Just before the buildings there is a stile and path on the left leading uphill. Go over the stile and up the path turning right where the path forks at the gateway. Continue uphill, through the thistle covered field to the gate onto a farm track. On the track turn right and walk to Bolton Hall Farm. As you reach the farm here is a wooden gate and stile on the left hand side. Go over the stile and across the field to the next stile. Follow the track, which leads left towards the woods on the other side.

There are good views on your left here of Preston with its tower blocks and church spires. You should also see your first lapwings. When I did this walk in July I couldn't walk far without their screeching cries warning me I was near their nest. These weren't the only wading birds I saw either. As I got nearer to Lancaster and Morecambe Bay I spotted several snipes, sandpipers and oyster catchers, all on their roosting areas from where they fly each day to feed on the flat sands and estuaries of the coast.

After the next stile follow the edge of the woods, downhill to the river-bank. Here turn left and follow the river downstream for $1/4$ mile to the weir.

Notice the Giant Hogweed growing on the opposite bank of the river Darwen. This enormous white flowered plant can grow up to 6ft and is often found by river banks. The plant was brought to this country by Victorian botanists. The whole plant is covered in tiny 'needles' which can give you a nasty sting which blisters up quite dramatically. You are lucky that these are on the opposite bank. When you come across them on an overgrown path it is useful to have a stick or a wife handy to bash them back and stop your legs getting blistered.

At the weir, go over the stile and follow the track across the field to the wooden gate and stile onto the road at Samlesbury Bottoms.

In earlier times this is where local folk brought their grain to be ground. The water mill has long since gone, as has the cotton mill built here in the early 19th century.

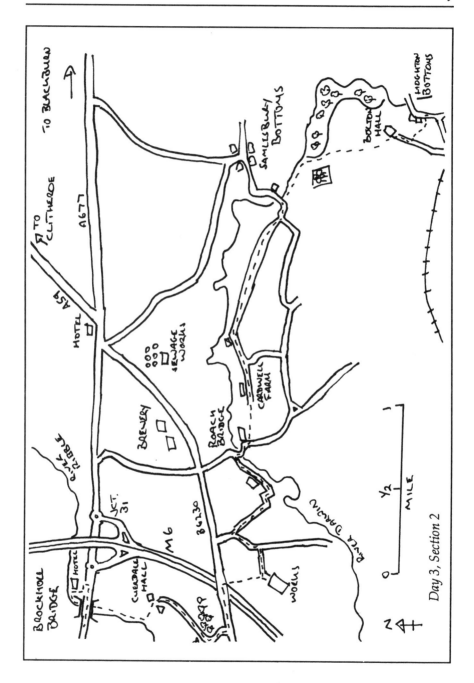

Day 3, Section 2

*No mills now, at Samlesbury Bottoms.*

On the road turn left and follow it uphill to the next road junction. Here turn right down Green Lane and continue for $3/4$ mile.

There are still, I am pleased to say, many hedgerows left in this part of the country. Hedges and hedgerows provide food and cover for many birds and small mammals. You can often find many plants here which are less common elsewhere. The older a hedge is the more plants you are likely to find. In fact, you can roughly tell how old a hedge is by the number of species which make up the hedge. This is how to do it. Start at any point along the hedge and walk 100 yards and as you do so, count the number of trees and shrubs which make up the hedge itself. Each species equals 100 years. So, if you just counted one plant, then it is a relatively young hedge of less than 100 years. Two species and the hedge is somewhere between 100-200 years old. This is only a rough guide but a fairly good indicator. See which is the oldest hedge you can find!

At the next road junction continue straight on following the sign to Cardwell's Farm. (Here you cross the Aqueduct again as it heads north to cross the Ribble. You can see the hump where it crosses the stream on your left.) Go through the farmyard and out through two metal gates to follow a track which leads to another metal gate. Carry on by an old field boundary to an overgrown stile and path. Follow this path down to the road.

At the road turn right and cross the river past Roach Bridge paper mill and turn immediately left down the lane signposted Cuerdale Lane. Follow this for $1/4$ mile to the farm. At the farm follow the footpath to the left of the farm, between the farm buildings and the river, and rejoin the track.

*Roach Bridge Paper Mill.*

Continue along the track to the road. On the road turn left and follow it for 300 yards, past the white house to the gate and green lane on the right. Turn right and follow this green lane to the works entrance. 20

yards before the work gates there is a stile on the right, partly hidden in the hedge. Go over this stile then bear left to the stile on the opposite side. Cross this and the next field to another stile and track which you follow to the main road (B6230). Turn left, cross the motorway and follow the road for $1/4$ mile to the public footpath sign on the right. Turn right and follow the track here through the woods to Cuerdale Hall Farm. Cross the farmyard and over the stone stile to follow the track opposite. At the tree with the wooden footpath notice after 30 yards turn right and follow the path by the river Ribble towards the main road. Go under the bridge into the hotel car park and up onto the main road. Turn right and cross Brockhole Bridge over the Ribble.

## Section 3. Brockhole Bridge to Longridge

A bridge was first built at this point on the river in 1824 for the Preston to Blackburn turnpike road. The bridge is still known locally as Halfpenny Bridge, since this was the cost to cross the bridge. It's a pity they didn't spend this money on strengthening the bridge because in August 1840 the bridge was swept away in a flood. The present bridge was built as a replacement in 1861.

Cross the bridge and turn immediately right down the lane on the opposite side of the river. After 150 yards the lane splits. Turn right here to follow the track towards the M6. Follow the track under the M6 and on for a further $3/4$ mile until the track leads into a field by some woods.

Ever since Cuerdale Hall Farm you have been following the route of the Ribble Way. This 72 mile walk follows the Ribble from its mouth near Preston to its source in Ribblesdale. The original route was first devised by the local Ramblers' Association in 1967. However, getting the path recognised proved very difficult since there were objections from local councils and farmers. So it wasn't until 1985 that the Ribble Way achieved official recognition.

In the field follow the blue Ribble Way signs to the left and up to the metal barriers by the woods. Turn left in the woods and walk to the top of the hill. Here turn right and follow the path by the edge of the woods to where the path forks at the end of the field. Here turn right again and past the two towers to continue on the path by the side of the woods. Eventually you will come to a stile on the right.

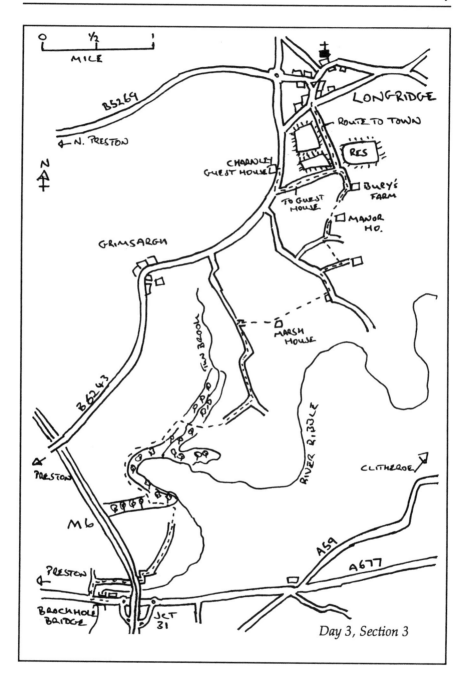

*Day 3, Section 3*

The edge of woods like this, are often used by birds for navigating and they will fly along the edge of the woods when travelling from area to area. When they get tired they will stop and rest. This gives them the chance to relieve themselves and they deposit a good amount of droppings on the way. These same droppings contain seeds from haws, blackberries and other fruit the bird has eaten. The seeds, surrounded by their own supply of fertiliser, quickly grow producing a layer of hawthorn and brambles around the edge of the wood. This distinct zone between one type of habitat and another is called an ecotone. Now there's something to impress your friends with! By the way, the pipeline along here is not the Thirlmere Aqueduct, which is further to the east, crossing the Ribble on a cast iron bridge made of three 70ft wide arches.

Go over the stile, following the Ribble Way signs and continue over 3 more stiles then right into the woods. Follow the path downhill through these delightful woods, cross the stream and back up the other side.

Look for the large yellow flowers of greater celandine here. This plant is a good indicator that the wood is pretty old, probably ancient (i.e. before 1600).

Go over the ladder stile and follow the Ribble Way sign to the right over the next ladder stile and onto the lane. Turn left and follow the lane for $1/4$ mile to the junction.

If you look over the hedge on your right, you should see a small, squat stone building. This is a well-head on the Thirlmere Aqueduct. When they built the Aqueduct, they wanted some way of controlling the flow, particularly in the cast iron pipelines which were prone to burst on occasions. So, whenever the Aqueduct changed from tunnel or cut and cover to pipeline, they built a North well with large valves to shut off the supply, and wherever the Aqueduct changed back from pipeline to cut and cover, a South well was built. By closing the valves in the North well, that section of pipeline could be cleared and any burst repaired. You will probably see several of these well-heads on the walk. This particular one is a North well where the Aqueduct changes from cut and cover to pipeline ready to cross the Ribble.

At the junction follow the road to the left (the Aqueduct is now just the other side of the hedge) and continue along the road for $3/4$ mile, past the sharp right and left bends to the farm track on the right (signposted Ribble Way). Follow this track, past the farms and onto the next Ribble Way sign. Follow the sign to the right, over the stone stile and across the field. Go straight across the next field, heading for the house opposite, and onto the road.

Turn left and follow the road for $1/4$ mile, passing the houses, to the road junction. Here turn right following the sign for Hothersall Lane, until you reach New Barn farmyard. Turn left opposite the last barn on the right and go over the stile on the other side of this small field. Cross the next field to the gate opposite and continue to the next gate and the farm lane.

Walk up the lane straight ahead to Manor Farm. At the farm turn left following the footpath sign painted on the wall and follow the track leading onto a bridleway between the overgrown hedges. Follow this bridleway, through the metal gate and by the hedge on the right into the farmyard. Follow the farm track, turning left at Bury's Farm, over the cattle grid and towards the reservoir embankments ahead.

> This series of reservoirs around Longridge were built to supply Longridge, Preston and other local towns with water.

At the junction of tracks by the small tower, you have a choice. If booked into Charnley House, turn left and follow this track to the main road (B6243), then turn right and the guest house is 200 yards on, on the left. If you have found accommodation in Longridge itself, continue straight on by the tower and the track brings you out by the church in the centre of Longridge.

> Whether you stay at the guest house or in the town itself, it is worth taking an evening stroll around Longridge (if your legs are up to it) if only to visit one of the several eating places. Longridge is another mill town, developed around a few cotton mills with many of the rows of terraced houses built for the mill workers. Longridge is, in fact, home to the oldest row of building society houses still standing anywhere in the world. Club Row (numbers 4-44 on Higher Road) were built in the 1790s by a group of quarry men

who formed a club and each paid one guinea a week to build the houses. As each house was completed the members drew lots to see who would move in, until all the row was finished. The houses are recorded in the Guinness Book of Records. The mills, the quarry and the railway which once ran here, have now all gone.

# DAY 4: LONGRIDGE TO DOLPHINHOLME

**Route:** Longridge – Beacon Fell – Brockmill – Calder Vale – Grizedale Fell – Dolphinholme.

**Distance:** 17 miles.

**Map:** O.S. Landranger 1:50,000 No.102 Preston and Blackpool.

**Getting There:** Longridge is 6 miles from Preston on the B6243. If you take this road out of Preston, leading to Clitheroe, the guest house and the start of today's walk is on the left, $1/2$ mile before you reach Longridge. By public transport the best way is by bus. There are several buses from Preston which run to either Clitheroe or Blackburn via Longridge. For example, 105 Preston to Clitheroe and 224 Preston to Blackburn. The nearest train station is Preston. For Dolphinholme see chapter 5.

**Accommodation:** The walk today ends in Dolphinholme – not quite a one horse town but certainly a one guest house town. This is the Old Mill House at Lower Dolphinholme. Once the old corn mill for the Lord of Wyreside, this pleasant and friendly guest house is reasonably priced and has the biggest four poster bed I have ever seen. However, they only have 3 rooms, so booking in advance is essential. The nearest alternative accommodation is at the Bay Horse off the A6, about 2 miles away:

The Old Mill House, Lower Dolphinholme, Near Lancaster, Lancs., LA2 9AX Tel. (0524) 791855.

# The Walk

Today's walk runs through the very heart of Lancashire. From Longridge you will cross rural landscapes where cows and lapwings abound. 'Farm-hopping' – passing from farm to farm on public footpaths – until you reach Beacon Fell Country Park with its picnic sites, car parks and brilliant views across to the Irish Sea. From there the walk takes you on a tour of small wooded valleys at the feet of the Forest of Bowland, each hiding its own little village or hamlet. After that it's out onto the open fell as you skirt round the foot of Grizedale Fell and then down to Dolphinholme on the River Wyre. A day of contrast and beauty, day 4 covers the largest distance as the crow flies and by the end of today you should really feel well on your way to reaching the end.

## Section 1. Longridge to Beacon Fell

From the town, walk down the main road (B6243) towards Preston until you reach the guest house on your right. From the guest house walk down the road away from Longridge for $1/4$ mile to the White Bull and public footpath sign on the right. Turn right and follow the track to the farm. Go through the farmyard and out on the track opposite. Continue across the next field to the wooden footbridge. Go over the bridge and continue straight on across the field towards the farm buildings $3/4$ mile ahead. Head for the left hand side of the buildings to find a ladder stile by a metal gate. Over this, cross the track and go through the gate opposite then over the stile on your left. Turn right to pass the next farm on your right to a metal gate and stile. After the stile head for a wooden bridge on your right. Cross the bridge, keeping a look-out for deer which often stray into the field from the nearby woods, then over the low fence and straight across the field onto a track running from left to right.

The instructions here sound complicated but work better 'in the field' so to speak. This is because the paths around here are little used and not signposted, so I want to send you the right way. If, however, you have time to look around you whilst following these directions, look over to your right where you can see the large mass of Longridge Fell dominating the view. This is where the town of Longridge gets its name and it's not difficult to see why the fell is so called. It is believed that Oliver Cromwell himself gave the fell its name, after he marched his army along the long-ridge to fight in the Battle of Preston during the Civil War. By the way, you have probably noticed another black gate here. Keep your eyes open and you should improve your score a bit more yet.

In the hedge in front of you is a wooden footbridge, sporting a yellow arrow. Cross this and along the right hand side of the next field to a red

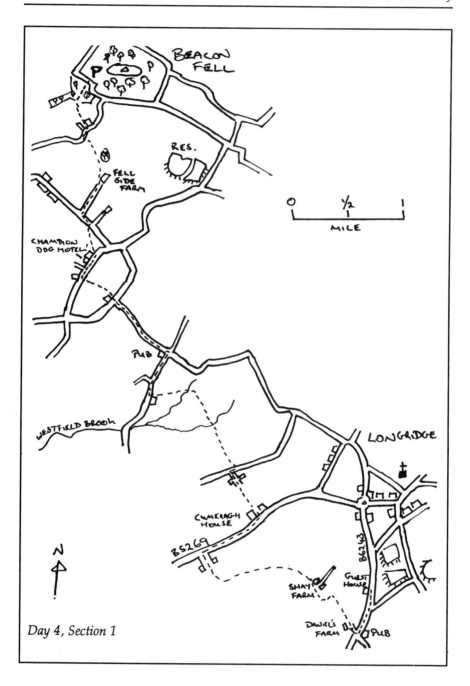

Day 4, Section 1

metal gate leading onto a hedged track. Follow the track for 75 yards, through another red gate and round to the left to two red metal gates opposite each other. Go through the gate on the right to follow the clear track to the Tomlinson's farm. Walk through the farmyard and out on the farm lane to the road. Turn right on the road and on for 200 yards to Cumeragh House Farm on the left. Between the house and the barn is a gate. Go through this, cross the yard and out of the gate opposite. Cross the field, over the stile and following the wire fence on your left, cross the next field to meet a track on the opposite side of the gateway. Follow this track until you reach a short, overgrown bridleway leading between two hedges, to a farm. (This bridleway was fenced off when I came this way, but it is a public right of way. Lancashire Council have promised to erect a stile here, so you should have no problems). Walk along this bridleway, through the farmyard to the road.

Here you will have a better view of Longridge Fell. Whether named by Cromwell or not, this long finger of sandstone provided the first industry for the town of Longridge. The first quarry was opened in 1830. The rich red sandstone quarried here was, in fact, used by Manchester Corporation as the facing stone for the Thirlmere Dam as well as all the other buildings along the Thirlmere Aqueduct. So, Longridge has its own special connection with this walk and when you finally reach the dam and see the stone, you will be able to remember this area where the stone was taken from.

Cross the road to pass through the metal gate on your right. Walk straight ahead, through the gate opposite and continue crossing the fields and over two stiles to a wooden gate on your right. Go through this, then left to the bottom of the field and a wooden footbridge over the stream. After the bridge, walk straight ahead across the large field for $1/4$ mile, heading for the obvious gap in the trees in the distance. Once at the gap you will come to a stream. Turn left and follow the stream to a wooden footbridge. Cross this and the stile opposite, then bear left to pass the only tree in the field, to another stile. Over this and straight ahead, to the left of the copse in the middle of the field and then by the left side of the house to the road. On the road turn right and continue for $1/2$ mile to the crossroads at the pub. Turn left and follow the road here for another $3/4$ mile to the T-junction and the farm opposite.

You may be feeling a little tired at this point, 3 days into the walk with 7 more to go, and your feet may be feeling weary, especially after that stretch of road walking. So I'll be kind to you and let you in on a little secret. Look along the hedgerows and roadsides as you continue your walk until you find some mugwort. This tall plant with its many-lobed leaves, which are silver underneath, and small ·white flowers, was once thought to have magical powers. The Romans recommended every traveller to carry a sprig of the plant, believing you would never become weary if you did so. So, take a little sprig, stick it down your boot and off you go, protected from all weariness and fatigue.

Here go through the wooden gate on the right of the farm, through the metal gate and then over the stile on the left by the slurry pit and cross to the fence. Follow the fence round to the wooden footbridge, then straight ahead over another footbridge and continue to the road opposite the house. Turn right and follow the road for 1/4 mile past Champion Dog Hotel and then the farm on the left. Immediately after the farm is a step-stile by a tree on the left. Go over this, through the gate opposite, then along the edge of the field to the metal gate on the far side. There is an old bathtub here and a stile on the right. Go over this and head for the diagonally opposite corner of the field to a stile and gate onto the road. Turn left along the road for 250 yards to a farm track on the right. Follow this track to Fell Side Farm.

It was at this farm that I met my first true Lancashire farmers. Two old men with hands and faces weathered by the elements, making it impossible to tell just how old they were. They watched me come up the track to the farm, silently leaning on their sticks with their faded cloth caps pushed back on their heads. When I asked where the footpath was, one of them pointed to the corner of the yard and told me where to go in the broadest, richest Lancashire accent I have ever heard.

In the far left hand corner of the farmyard is a small wooden gate by a green shed. Go through this and follow the edge of the field, over two stiles and continue to a gate onto the road. Turn right on the road and walk uphill, past the first house on the left. Then turn left up the track between the houses and into the field. Bear left uphill to the gate. Go through this, then turn left and contour round the hill to a small gorge.

Follow this uphill to a stile into the woods. In the woods, follow the path
to the car park and road. This is Beacon Fell Country Park and there are
toilets here by the car park.

## Section 2.Beacon Fell to Grizedale Fell.

Beacon Fell was bought by Lancashire County Council in 1969
with the specific purpose of attracting tourists and taking some of
the pressure off the Forest of Bowland. Beacon Fell Country Park
is now this small wooded hill with several car parks, picnic sites
and nature trails laid out for visitors to enjoy this small piece of
Lancashire. There are good views from here and the information
board by the car park will tell you more.

On the road turn left and follow it for $1/4$ mile to the sharp right bend.
Here turn left over a stile and into a field. Follow the clear path downhill
to the road. Turn right, then left at the junction (unsuitable for heavy
vehicles) and continue on this road for $3/4$ mile to Brockmill at the
bottom of the valley.

As you walk, you can continue your search for mugwort (and black
gates!) along the tree-lined verges of this quiet lane. Though I can't
guarantee mugwort, you should spot some garlic mustard plants,
with its heart shaped leaves and small, white flowers. A common
hedgerow plant, its leaves have a wonderful oniony flavour which
goes very well in a salad or just to chew on their own (make sure
you have the right plant first!). It is not hard to see how this plant
got its name. What about the tall, purple fox-gloves that can also
be seen along here? How did that get its name? Well, in ancient
times it was believed that putting the long, bell-shaped flowers on
your fingers made you as wily as a fox. This is not something I
would recommend, since you may put your finger in to find a big
bumble bee already there!

At the bottom of the vale, cross the two bridges then turn left to follow
the signpost for Walmsley Bridge. Follow the path by the river for $1/4$
mile to another signpost. Turn right following the Brockmill Lane sign,
to walk uphill, through the woods, to the road. Turn left, and after $1/4$
mile you will approach a junction in the road. 100 yards before the
junction, turn right through a wooden 5-bar gate. Cross the field and

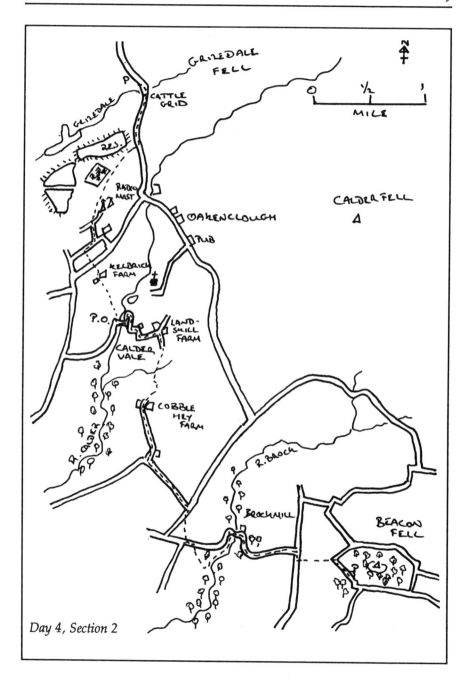

Day 4, Section 2

ditch and then bear left to a metal gate. Go onto the track here and follow this to the road. Go right, then first left along the road signposted for Garstang. Continue for $1/2$ mile to the sharp left bend. Turn right up the farm track here, past the first farm, and continue on the track round to the left for another $1/2$ mile to Cobble Hey Farm.

Notice the old stone drinking trough at the farm as well as the odd black gate, or two.

Go through the cobbled farmyard and turn right at the end, into the field. Follow the track with the wall on your right until you reach a metal gate. Do NOT go through this gate, but turn left and walk downhill to another metal gate on your right. Go through this, over the small stream, then bear left to yet another metal gate in the far corner of this field. Pass through this gate and follow the overgrown bridleway to Landskill Farm.

When I came this way in July, the mole catcher had been at work and the products of his labour were on display. Tiny, black moles were pinned in a line to the fence as proof to the farmer that the mole catcher had earned his pay.

In the farmyard, turn left and follow the farm track downhill, through the next farm, then left and downhill again to Calder Vale. Walk past the row of terraced houses (Long Row) and Methodist church and turn right over the bridge.

Calder Vale was built as a model village by the Jackson brothers in the 1830s. Richard and Jonathan Jackson were two Quaker brothers who saw the horrors and poverty of backstreet Manchester and wanted to build their own cotton mills, where the workers would be happy and well cared for. They built two mills here in this secluded valley in 1835 using the River Calder as their power source. They then built the terraced houses to house the workers, each worker with his own house and each house with its own garden. This was their model village. In its heyday all the women in the Vale were skilled weavers at the mill and all the menfolk worked at the paper mill at Oakenclough set up by John Jackson, another of the brothers. Being Quakers, there is no pub in the Vale, but there was once a Temperance Hotel, along with three other shops and a chippie. Today only the Post Office is left, though one of the mills is still in use, just here by the bridge, and Calder Vale remains a thriving community.

*Long Row Terrace, Caldervale*

After the bridge, turn right at the post office, then left to follow the public footpath sign up the slightly overgrown path (which soon clears) through the woods. When you come out of the woods at the top, bear right and follow the track, which becomes clearer further on, leading to Kelbrick Farm. Pass through the farmyard and round to the left, following the track down to the road. Cross the road and through the metal gate opposite. Cross the field and go over the stile onto a grass track. Turn right and follow the track to Bank Farm.

Just before the farmyard, turn left at the metal gate and follow another grass track to a tarmac lane by the radio masts. Cross the lane and walk up the track opposite which bears right, past the radio masts. Continue past the plantation and reservoirs on the left, to meet the road. On the road turn left and follow the road for $^1/_2$ mile to the cattle grid.

# Section 3. Grizedale Fell to Dolphinholme

Grizedale Fell is the large fell on your right and is one of the many fells which make up the vast Forest of Bowland. The Forest of Bowland is a large range of steep sided hills and fells covered in a vast expanse of heather moorland, which takes up most of the north-east corner of Lancashire. The area is the same now as it was when the Normans first called this moorland a 'Forest', meaning a hunting area, although all the truly wild deer have gone. The area is still used for hunting today but the prey, now, is red grouse rather than red deer. Most of the land is privately owned and managed for this purpose and is closed to the public. However, there is access to certain parts and tomorrow we get the chance to cross our first true fell.

After the cattle grid, then turn left by the small layby to follow the bridleway sign. Follow the bridleway which contours around the hill to Fell End Farm. Go into the farmyard and turn right at the house, up through the metal gate into the field. There is no clear path here so bear left and head for the top corner of the plantation 200 yards away. When you reach the plantation, continue in a straight line until you reach the road. You should come out on the road by a public footpath sign. Cross the road and follow a similar sign on the opposite side. Follow the direction of the sign along a path which contours around the side of the fell. This indistinct path through the heather, little more than a sheep track at times, remains on the same level around the hill for nearly a mile, crossing a stream and then on towards another.

As you walk this path, you will be walking through a typical moorland vegetation of heathers, bilberries and sheep's fescue. Heather is the staple diet of the grouse, which are breed for shooting in these parts, but being the fussy little birds they are, they will only eat the new growth. For this reason, on land managed for grouse shooting, the heather is burnt every 10-15 years to encourage new growth. Plants such as bilberry cannot tolerate this burning, so will only grow in abundance where the land is not managed in this way. Bilberries will also only grow on drier parts of the moor. So, by looking at the plants around, you can tell how the land is used and the type of soil it is on.

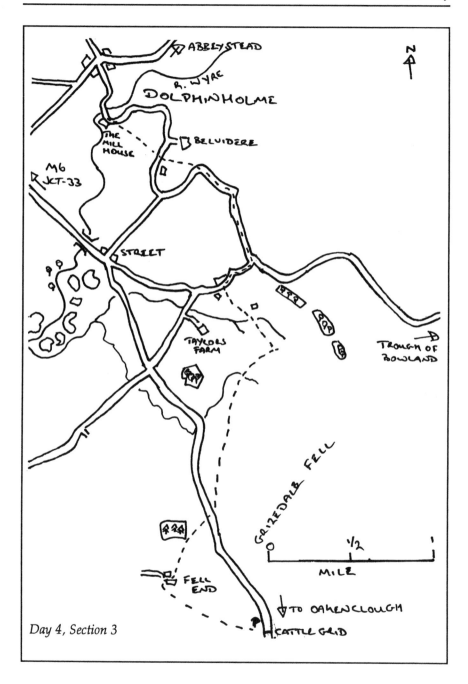

*Day 4, Section 3*

After nearly 1 mile on this path you will now be heading west and below you on your left, you will see white farm buildings and small woods. At this point turn left and, heading for Heysham power station (the large square block) on the coast, make your way downhill until you reach a wall or wire fence. Turn right and follow the wall (which will become a wire fence, if not already) or fence until you reach a stile over the fence. The stile lies, in the corner, next to a large holly bush.

As you made your way downhill, you will have crossed the Thirlmere Aqueduct for the seventh time today. As the Aqueduct has contoured along the edge of the Forest of Bowland, roughly following the 500ft contour level, you have been zig-zagging across its course. You can imagine the problem the Victorian engineers would have faced in this area, where the line will have travelled under high moorland hills bisected by deep river valleys. I hope you made the most of today to increase your gate score. From now on we shall only cross the Aqueduct once or twice in any day.

Go over the stile and continue downhill between the fence and the small stream on your right. Follow this path, which becomes a track, across the stream to meet with another track by some old farm buildings to the right. Turn left here and follow the track downhill for $1/4$ mile to the road. Turn right on the road and walk for $1/4$ mile to the junction by the white railings. Turn left down the small lane and follow this for $1/2$ mile, past the white house on the right, to where the road bends sharply left in a large curve. Here go through the metal 7-bar gate on the right and turn left to follow the edge of the field to the step stile by the trees. Go over this and head left towards the house. Walk around the back of the walled house to the road.

Cross the road and the wooden footbridge opposite, then bear right across the field to a stile. Follow the path, through the kissing-gate, and onto the next stile into the field. Bear left here to the diagonally opposite corner of the field and a small metal ladder by a ruined chimney (or it could be an old tower – I couldn't tell which). Go over the ladder and follow the path through the woods to the road at Lower Dolphinholme. Turn left and the Old Mill House is 150 yards on, just before you reach the bridge. Head inside for a warm welcome and well earned rest.

*Lower Dolphinholme and a Night's Rest.*

# DAY 5: DOLHINHOLME TO CATON

**Route:** Dolphinholme – Jubilee Tower – Grit Fell – Littledale – Caton.

**Distance:** 11 miles.

**Maps:** O.S. Landranger 1:50,000 No.102 Preston and Blackpool. O.S. Landranger 1:50,000 No. 97 Kendal to Morecambe.

**Getting There:** Dolphinholme and the start of the walk at Lower Dolphinholme, are just 5 minutes by car, from Junction 33 of the M6. Come off the motorway here onto the A6 and turn left towards Preston. After just 25 yards, turn left again down a small lane to a T-junction. Turn right and along this road for just over 1 mile to a crossroads at the Fleece Inn. Turn left at the inn and follow this road into Dolphinholme. At the mini-roundabout in Dolphinholme, turn right and down the lane into Lower Dolphinholme. If coming from Preston or Lancaster, follow the A6 to Junction 33 of the M6 and then follow these same instructions.

There are only two buses to Dolphinholme, both of which run from Lancaster to Abbeystead. These are the 146 and the 147 and are fairly infrequent, so it is worth checking times. The nearest train station is at Lancaster. For Caton, see chapter 6.

**Accommodation:** Caton, though considerably larger than Dolphinholme, again only boasts one guest house. This is on the main road from Lancaster to Kirkby Lonsdale (A683). There may be other accommodation at nearby Brookhouse. The accommodation at Caton is York Villa, a cheap and comfortable guest house:

York Villa Guest House, 34 Hornby Road, Caton, Near Lancaster, Lancs.. Tel. (0524) 770845.

There is plenty of alternative accommodation in Lancaster, 15 minutes away by bus, should York Villa be full.

# The Walk

Two things to celebrate on today's walk. Firstly, the only true fell summit on the whole walk and secondly, the halfway point of the walk. The fact that both these important milestones occur, not only on the same day, but at the same point, must be put down to good luck rather than good planning. It still calls for breaking open a bottle of ginger beer on the top of Grit Fell – 1,530 ft above sea level and $68^1/_2$ miles along the Thirlmere Way.

The walk itself? Well, it consists of 3 parts. The walk across rural farmland to Grit Fell, the walk over Grit Fell and the walk across Littledale away from Grit Fell. The first real wilderness, the first real get-away-from-the-world feeling, the first real navigation problems all occur today.

Grit Fell is one of the outlying fells of the Forest of Bowland and is owned and used by shooting people. The only reason you are allowed to walk over it, is due to Lancashire County Council negotiating access with the owners. However, at certain times the fell is strictly out of bounds (unless you want to be mistaken for a grouse) and it is obviously worthwhile finding out when this is before you set off. To do this ring the Access Area Warden on Garstang (09952) 2784, who should be able to tell you well in advance. Even if you check before you start the Thirlmere Way, it is worth checking again on the day in question since they are sometimes sneaky and close off the area with little warning. If this happens and you find you can't walk that day, you have two alternatives.

Get the bus into Lancaster and spend a day looking around this historic town before returning to Dolphinholme to start the walk tomorrow; or instead, get the bus into Lancaster and spend a day looking around this historic town before bussing out to Caton and missing out Day 4 completely. Or I suppose you could give up completely and go home, but I'm sure you wouldn't do that, would you?

## Section 1. Dolphinholme to Jubilee Tower

Dolphinholme itself is actually a small village at the top of the hill. The Old Mill House where you stayed last night is part of Lower Dolphinholme, which I suppose is the original Dolphinholme. Until the end of the 18th century Dolphinholme consisted of Dolphinholme Farm, the corn mill itself and Wyreside Hall, a large house further downstream. The village expanded with the building of a Worsted spinning mill, built to use the power of the River Wyre. The mill once boasted the second largest water-wheel in Britain (after the Laxey Wheel on the Isle of Man). When the mill closed in 1867 the 68ft wheel was blown up. The name Dolphinholme, by the way, comes from the time of the Vikings, when a Norse called Dolfin chose this site by the Wyre for his settlement or holme.

On the road outside the Mill House, turn right and walk up the road for $1/2$ mile to the farm track to Dolphinholme House Farm on the left. Follow this tarmac lane, taking the farm track at the bend, and continue for $1/2$ mile to where this track bends sharp right. Go straight ahead, through a wooden 5-bar gate and follow the grass track with the fence on your right. (Note what look like bin lids stuck in the ground. These are inspection chambers on the Thirlmere Aqueduct.)

When you reach a metal gate, go through it and bear slightly right to cross the field heading for a stone barn ahead. Pass this barn and follow the old field boundary to a metal 7-bar gate. Go through this gate and head up to the farm ahead. Pass behind the farm, through the metal gate, then bear left to the corner of the wood opposite. Go over the step stile here into the plot of newly planted trees. Turn right and follow the path leading down through the woods to the river. Follow the river upstream to an iron and wooden footbridge. Cross the bridge, through the kissing gate and over the ladder stile opposite. Walk up the steps, over another stile and uphill following the fence on your right.

Where the fence bends sharply right, bear slightly right and walk uphill, parallel with the fence, to the stile at the top. Now follow the yellow arrows round the field and over the stile into the farmyard at Lentworth Hall.

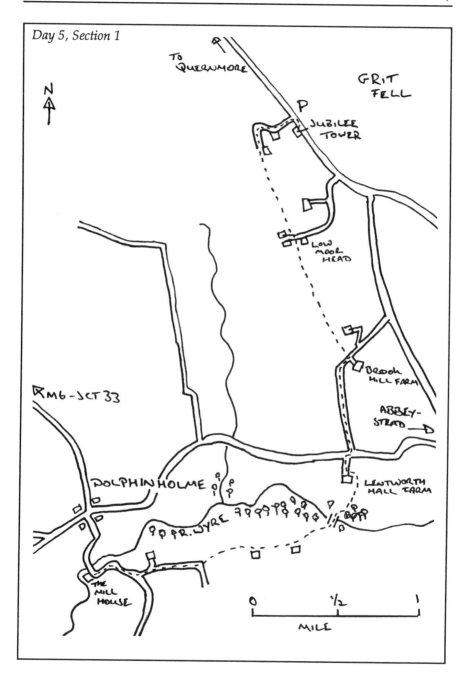

Day 5, Section 1

*Bridge over Wyre, Nr Dolphinholme.*

This is one of the many farmyards on this walk where the only thing that seems to abound is slurry. Most of the farms, and indeed farm tracks, have had a generous spread of slurry across them. At one point I even considered calling the walk 'The Slurry Trail, a tour of Lancashire's highest places'. I don't think this has the same appeal though.

Walk across the farmyard and follow the track ahead to the tarmac lane. Turn right and follow the lane, cross the main road and up to the main road opposite. Follow this lane for $1/2$ mile to the entrance of Brook Hill Farm on the right. Turn left here through the wooden kissing gate. Follow the edge of the field, with the fence on your right, through several gates until you come to Low Moor Head Farm after $1/2$ mile. Cross the farm track, over the stone stile opposite and now follow the fence on your left.

Watch out for the dive-bombing house martins! They are not after you but after the low flying insects that are buzzing around. The birds fly about, scooping up any insect reckless enough to get in the way. They will often fly just over your head and although I've never been hit by a house martin or swift, they have come very close once or twice.

Continue to follow the fence on your left, heading for the stone house in the distance. At the second field boundary go over the stile on your left by the stream, then turn right so that the fence is now on your right. Go over the step stile in the corner and continue straight ahead towards the stone house. At the house go over the stone stile and follow the track straight ahead which bends around to the right, past the farmyard and up to the road by Jubilee Tower.

## Section 2. Jubilee Tower to Littledale

Jubilee Tower was built by James Harrison for Queen Victoria's Golden Jubilee in 1887. It is worth climbing for the increased view it provides; a taste of things to come as you climb Grit Fell. It also provides some protection from the elements behind its mock ramparts – enough for you to study your map without it blowing off into the distance. Across from the tower is a small car park with a plaque about the 7th century coffin found on this site when the car park was built. It's worth reading before you set off.

From the car park follow the clear path straight ahead, up the moor. The path follows the fence on the right for $1^1/_4$ miles to the large stone pillar at the top. This is Shooter's Pile (a landmark – not a medical condition!).

Now is the time to crack open the bottle of lemonade as you reach the exact halfway mark on the walk. This gives you time to look at the vegetation around you. There is much more bilberry here than yesterday, showing how much drier the ground is (though you probably wouldn't believe it after walking up that hill). Also time to take in the fantastic view to the west. Looking out towards Lancaster you can quite clearly see the Lune Estuary, Morecambe Bay and the great square block of Heysham Power Station. Beyond this, the Lake District with Arnside and Grange on the coast and the hills beyond. A glimpse of things to come.

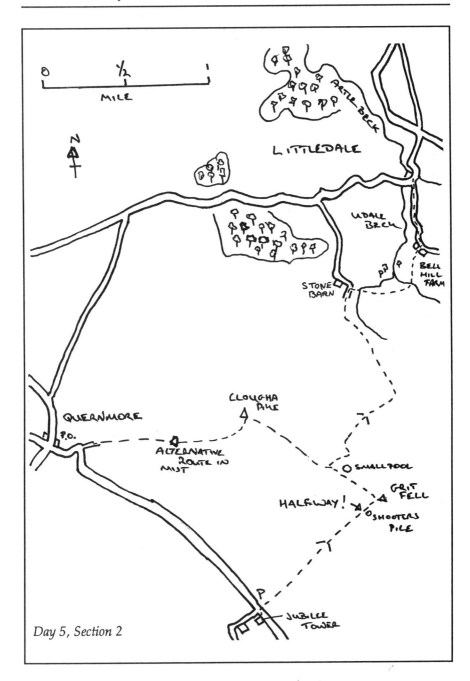

Day 5, Section 2

From the stone pile continue by the fence to the stile by the notice board. Do not go over this but turn left and follow the path with the fence on your right to another stile. Cross this and follow the clearly cairned, peaty path to a small pool on the right after a third of a mile. Continue on the path for another 100 yards and look carefully for a small cairn 5 yards from the path on the right. Walk to this cairn from where you will spot another just ahead. Continue to follow these cairns past two small pools and head for a clearer path straight ahead.

> This path which goes off to the right and down to Littledale is difficult to find even in the best of conditions and should you be caught in the mist it's not worth trying. Instead continue on the main path from Grit Fell which leads over Clough Pike then downhill to Quernmore. At Quernmore turn right past the post office and walk along the road to Littledale (see map). It may be harder on the feet, but it's better than being lost on the moors.

The path to Littledale gradually becomes clearer and stonier, often becoming a small stream at times, as it winds its way downhill through the heather. Continue on this path for $1^1/_2$ miles until it meets a stream by a wall. Keeping the stream on your right, follow it downhill to a ladder stile. Cross this and then right following the trees down to where a walled track goes off to the left to a stone barn. Turn right here to cross the stream in the trees and carry on ahead following the wire fence on your right, to a wooden 5-bar gate. Go through this and turn left walking downhill to a wooden footbridge. After the bridge go through the metal gate and walk uphill to Bellhill Farm. In the farmyard turn left and follow the track heading downhill towards the valley. Follow this track for $1/_2$ mile to the road.

> Notice all the small blue flowers of self-heal by the track, as well as the pale blue bells of the harebell. Self-heal gets its name from its ancient reputation to cure almost everything. In fact Gerard, the Elizabethan herbalist, says that an infusion of self-heal and wine "doth make whole and sound all wounds both inward and outward." . Modern herbalists recommend it as a gargle for sore throats. In Scotland the harebell is known as the bluebell and the bluebell as wild hyacinth. So if you are Scottish you now know what I am talking about.

## Section 3. Littledale to Caton

My original intention when planning the walk was to take a clear path which leads across the hills on your left down into Caton. However, when walking this way I was firmly turned back and informed that it was private land and the paths were used only by shooting parties. So, if you happen to be carrying a shotgun then you could probably head that way. Otherwise you will have to come with me along the road.

On the road go straight ahead over the large stone bridge and follow the road uphill, past the scout camp and onto the house at the road junction. Here follow the track straight ahead, to the right of the houses. Continue on this track for $1/2$ mile until it remeets the road.

This should be easier than when I did the walk and met several dozen sheep travelling in the opposite direction. Not one to argue, I stepped aside whilst this mobile road-block went on its way.

*A Road Block!*

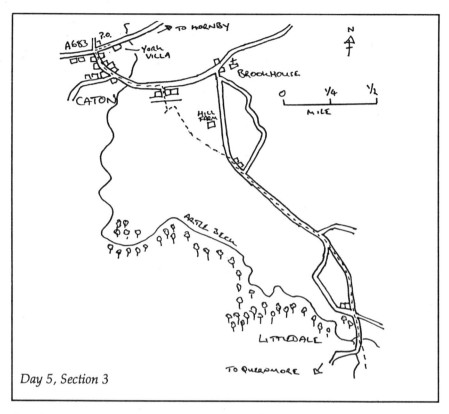

Day 5, Section 3

Continue straight ahead on the road for 3/4 mile to the houses by the
road junction. Continue for another 100 yards to the second metal
signpost on the left (with the little man on). Follow the sign through the
iron kissing gate then bear right to the far corner and the step stile in the
fence on the right. Go over this and straight ahead to the opposite fence.
Cross this and walk straight ahead over the small hill to a metal gate on
the opposite side. Pass the gate on your left to a stile in the corner of the
field. Go over the stile and walk downhill to the path behind the houses.
Turn left on the path and follow the fence for 100 yards to an iron
kissing gate on your right. Go through this and cross the field to the
road. Follow the road to the main road and turn left towards Caton
(Brookhouse is to the right). Follow this road for 1/2 mile to the junction
with the main A683 by the petrol station. Turn right along the A683 and
York Villa is 200 yards along on the right.

# DAY 6. CATON TO KIRKBY LONSDALE

**Route:** Caton – Crook O'Lune – Gressingham – Hill Top – Hutton Roof – Kirkby Lonsdale.

**Distance:** 16 miles.

**Map:** O.S. Landranger 1:50,000 No. 97 Kendal to Morecambe.

**Getting There:** Caton is 5 miles from Lancaster on the A683 road to Hornby and Kirkby Lonsdale. York Villa is on the main road and is easy to spot. If coming from the motorway, junction 34 leads straight on to the A683 – just follow the signs for Hornby and Kirkby Lonsdale. Caton is about 3$^1$/$_2$ miles from the junction. There are several buses which run between Lancaster and Caton including the 280, 276, 277 and 278, the last 3 of which also run to Kirkby Lonsdale. For Kirkby Lonsdale see chapter 7.

**Accommodation:** Today, and on the rest of the walk, you will have a wealth of choice when it comes to finding somewhere to stay. Kirkby Lonsdale is very much a tourist town and provides coffee shops, gift shops and bed and breakfasts in abundance. For this reason I have not recommended any one guest house but have directed you instead to the Tourist Information Centre. Whenever you go, you should be able to find somewhere to stay, but if you wish to have a room booked before you set off, then the address of the Tourist Information Centre is given below:

Kirkby Lonsdale Tourist Information Centre, 24 Main Street, Cumbria LA6 2AE Tel. (05242) 71437.

As I said in the introduction Kirkby Lonsdale was actually my second choice for the night's stop, Hutton Roof being my first. However, the only accommodation in Hutton Roof is provided by the caravan and camp site near the church. So if you are one of those brave souls who carries their own accommodation on your back, you can pitch your gear at Hutton Roof and do the 'original Thirlmere Way' which has the advantage of being 4 miles shorter.

# The Walk

Truly a splendid walk today, possibly my favourite of the whole walk. If you buy this book and never do the whole walk, at least go and do Day 6 otherwise you will have really missed out. The first part of the walk is spent following the banks of the Lune through ancient woodlands full of wild flowers and the chance to see kingfishers and otters if you're lucky. You are then taken through the pretty village of Gressingham and across the border into Cumbria. Here the scenery changes as the underlying rock changes to limestone and the difference can be clearly seen in the many dry stone walls. From Hutton Roof the walk leads back down into the valley and the town of Kirkby Lonsdale where you can treat yourself to afternoon tea for a perfect end to the day.

# Section 1. Caton to Gressingham

Caton with Littledale, together with nearby Brookhouse, lay claim to a population of around 3000. Most of these are commuters to nearby Lancaster, but 200 years ago Caton had its own industry with 8 cotton and wood turning mills. Because of its position at the entrance to the Lune valley and its closeness to Lancaster, Caton has always been an important site even in Roman times. This was proved in 1803 when a 6ft high Roman milestone was found buried here.

From the guest house walk along the A683 back to the junction by the pub and garage. Here turn right past the post office to the catholic church. Pass the church and walk to the wooden kissing gate on the left. Go through this and follow the path along the disused railway line.

This railway, built in 1849 between Lancaster and Wennington, was closed with the Beeching cuts in 1966. The line has now been turned into 'Caton footpath' which abounds with information boards telling you about the line and also Low Mill, one of the mills left standing, though no longer in use.

Follow the path for $1/2$ mile through several kissing gates to cross the river on a metal bridge.

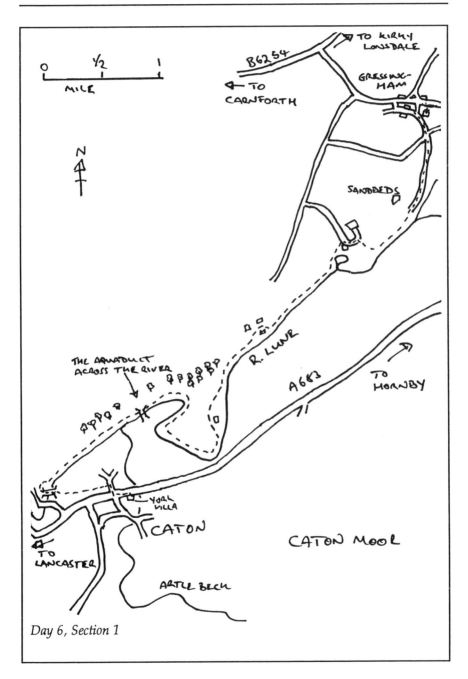

Day 6, Section 1

This is the Crook O'Lune – an important crossing point of the river Lune, made famous by Turner in his painting of the river here.

*The road bridge over the Lune, Caton.*

Immediately after the bridge turn right down the path to the river. Follow this path with the river on your right for just over 1 mile through woods and fields until you come to the massive bridge which carries the Thirlmere Aqueduct across the river in 4 large pipes.

As I walked along this first stretch of river I knew that there were ramsons in the wood somewhere, because I could smell them quite strongly. That strong garlic smell is unmistakeable, but it was a while before I realised that only the dead flower heads were left and the flowers had long since gone to seed. The plant's broad leaves, designed for catching as much light as possible, were still visible though. When young, the leaves can be used in salads or to flavour soups and stews, though not too much since the garlic flavour is very strong. It is said that if cows eat the leaves, their milk will taste of garlic. Not a pleasant thought.

Just beyond the woods is the point where the Thirlmere Aqueduct crosses the river Lune in the form of 4 mighty cast iron pipes. You can see the pipes quite clearly as you walk underneath them. Yes, underneath them! Up until now you have crossed the Aqueduct several times, with the black gates showing where the water was flowing some way beneath you. This is the first and last chance you have of walking directly underneath the pipeline with the water flowing several feet above your head on its way to Manchester. Listen carefully and you might even hear it!

Pass the Aqueduct and continue on the path by the river back into the woods where bluebells can be seen (sorry, wild hyacinths if you're Scottish). You come out of the woods into a field where the river bends off to the right.

From here, looking up the valley you should be able to see the famous flat top of Ingleborough Fell in the distance. This great outcrop of limestone pavement forms one of the 3 peaks along with Whernside and Pen-y-gent.

Continue to follow the path by the river until it leads onto a track leading back towards the woods and then past an old stone barn and houses. Ignore the 'River 1/4 mile' sign here but go on another 20 yards to the barn and stile on the right. Here turn right past the barn and on the track back to the riverside.

You will now be able to see Hornby Castle with its mock embattlements and turrets sitting quite happily below Ingleborough. This piece of Victorian architecture is built around a 13th century Pele Tower, built originally as protection from marauding Scots (probably in search of wild hyacinths).

Continue on the path by the river for 1 mile to the track by the house. Here turn right, over the cattle grid and on 100 yards to a wooden 5-bar gate with a yellow arrow on. Go through the gate and along the path to the left, which skirts the bottom of the hill with the house on, until you reach the ornate iron gate leading onto the road. Follow the road uphill for 3/4 mile to Gressingham.

## Section 2. Gressingham to Henridding Farm

Gressingham is a small but ancient village, mentioned in the Doomsday Book. The church here is Saxon in origin, though many of the houses in the village date from the Stuart period.

Cross the small stone bridge on the right and pass the church to the main road. Turn left, then quickly right up the minor road and follow this for $1/2$ mile to where the road bends sharply left. Go through a wooden gate on the right at this point and bear left towards the corner of the woods opposite, to a stile. After the stile bear right to the next stile. Go over this and then straight ahead to another stile into the trees and onto the road. Turn right on the road, past Storrs Hall, to the road junction. Turn left down Locka Lane and follow this for 1 mile to an old white house on the left hand bend.

Along this lane you can continue your search for mugwort started on Day 4, though if you have not found any by now, it's probably too late. Mugwort, by the way, gets its name from its reputation for getting rid of small flies. Mug is a short version of midge and wort means healer – so mugwort – 'midgehealer'. The wort part is found in many plants such as butterwort (used to help churn butter), stitchwort (used to heal wounds) and milkwort (used for nursing mothers). Some names, however, remain a mystery. Take hedge parsley. A common enough plant – you will probably see its white 'parasol' flower-heads and parsley-like leaves along the lane. Its name obviously comes from its leaves. Why then, in some parts of the country, is it known as welcome-home-husband-though-never-so-drunk? This is a name used only in the south of the country, which explains quite a lot about the people who live there.

Continue on the road for another 100 yards after the white house to where the road bends sharply right then left.On the right here is a stone stile. Cross the stile and head downhill to a gap in the wall on the opposite side of the field. Go through this and head between the two sets of trees, bearing right after a while to follow the edge of the trees on that side. With the trees on your right, walk down to the stream and gate. Pass through the gate and then left to the tarmac track. Cross the track and piece of grass to the stone pillars in the wall. Squeeze between the pillars and walk straight on across the field to the gate onto the road.

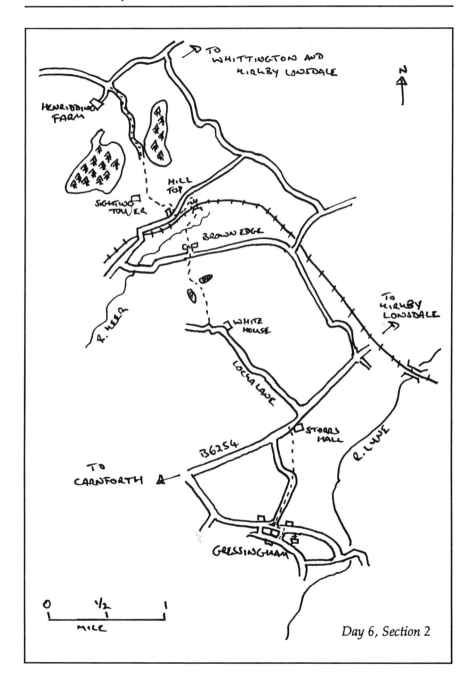

Day 6, Section 2

Cross the road by Brown Edge Farm and follow the farm track through the farmyard and metal gate. Continue on the track towards the power lines. Pass under the buzzing lines and to a wooden footbridge on the left. Cross the bridge and bear right to the subway under the railway in the opposite corner. Go under the railway and then turn left to skirt around the field and up onto the lane opposite Hill Top Farm

> This farm has the biggest, noisiest and most ferocious dog in any of the farmyards on this walk. Luckily the path does not go through the farmyard and the dog's chain is only long enough to let it reach the farm gate. Perhaps the dog is a border guard since it is here that you leave Lancashire behind and cross into Cumbria for the final 52 miles.

On the road turn right, then left up the side of the farm to pass through the wooden gate and follow the track round to the left and behind the farm. Head uphill, bearing slightly left heading for the stone tower on the hill.

> The tower is a sighting tower built by the Manchester engineers to help sight the exact line of the Thirlmere Aqueduct. There are many of these towers up and down the line, but this is the only one we shall get to see close-up. It is also a chance to increase your gate score – so keep your eyes open!

Pass through the gate and continue uphill to the crest of the hill near to the tower.

> From here you can see the massive coat of arms of Manchester carved into the side of the stonework.

From the top of the hill bear right, keeping the tower on your left, to the edge of the woods about $1/4$ mile away on the top of another small hill. At the woods turn left and follow the edge of the woods, with the trees on your right, to a track. Follow the track, which leads uphill, for $3/4$ mile to the road by Henridding Farm.

# Section 3. Henridding Farm to Kirkby Lonsdale

Turn right on the road and follow it for $1/2$ mile to the road junction.

The hill on your left, as you walk along this road, is Hutton Roof crags, a classical example of a limestone pavement. The river Lune roughly divides the area into limestone to the north and gritstone to the south. You can tell the difference here in the dry stone walls which are much whiter than those you have seen so far on this walk.

Continue on the road for another 250 yards to Crag House Farm on the left. Turn left up the lane here and follow it through the farmyard. At the end of the yard go through the wooden gate on the left and follow the green track and the edge of the woods on the left. Keeping the old hawthorn hedge (now fully grown trees) on your left continue straight across the field on a faint track for $1/2$ mile to a stone stile by the corner of some woods.

The Aqueduct runs parallel with the walk here, some 200 yards to your right. When the line reaches Hutton Roof it turns off to the west towards Kendal and the Lakes, whereas you turn east towards Kirkby Lonsdale and a bed.

Go over the stile and follow the clear path by the information board onto a track. Turn left on the track and follow this to down to the road. On the road turn left and walk $1/4$ mile to the road junction near the post office at Hutton Roof.

Hutton Roof. $1^{1}/_{2}$ miles from Lupton and $252^{1}/_{4}$ miles from London. How do I know this? Because of the old yellow A.A. sign on the local garage. This old sign, some 40 years old, is probably the most modern thing in Hutton Roof, a beautiful little village of limestone cottages caught in time.

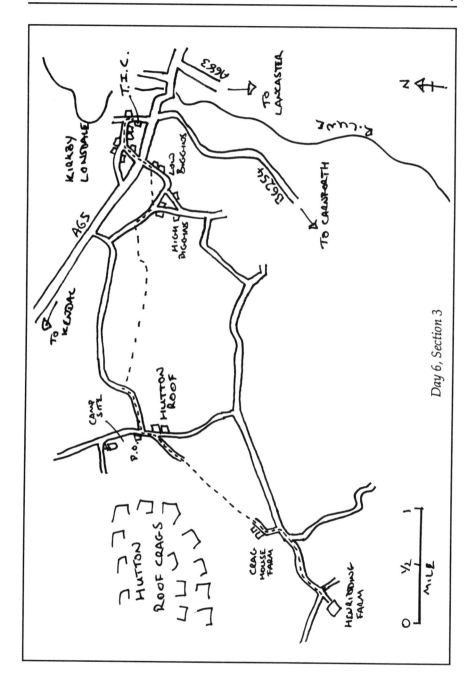

*Day 6, Section 3*

Hutton Roof has one claim to fame as far as this walk goes – the Mission Hall here was built especially for the navvies who worked on the Aqueduct and were based in the village.

The building of the dam at Thirlmere and the Aqueduct itself meant a large workforce had to be brought into the Lake District and various towns along the route. The largest number of men were based in the Lakes and caused enormous social problems. Temporary accommodation in the form of huts, had to be built for them. When some of the workmen's children were found wandering the mountains with nothing to do, Manchester Corporation built temporary schools and mission halls which were also used as libraries and soup kitchens when the snow stopped work in the winter. Hutton Roof was used as a base for this part of the Aqueduct, which runs round the bottom of Hutton Roof Crags. The men were housed on local farms and in huts in the village. A mission hall was also built and when the men left, the hall stayed and is still standing to this day.

At the junction turn right down the road signposted Kirkby Lonsdale. (Notice the Cumbria Cycle Path sign as well. This is a long distance cycle path which follows the Cumbrian border.) Follow the road for $1/4$ mile to the wooden signpost on the right. Turn right and follow the sign for Kirkby Lonsdale uphill to 2 gates.

Go through the gate on the left and following the overhead power lines, cross 2 fields to reach a stone stile. Go over this and continue to follow the power lines downhill to a metal gate and track. Go through the gate and follow the track for 50 yards to a metal gate off to the left, with a blue arrow on it. Turn left, through the gate, and follow the path uphill to a gateway on the right. After the gateway, continue straight ahead along the edge of the field to a gap in the wall opposite. Follow the blue arrow left after the gap, on the path across the field to a metal gate. Go through the gate and the gap opposite to cross the final field and onto the road.

On the road turn right and on for $1/4$ mile to the footpath sign on the left for Low Biggins. Follow the sign and the path through the woods and across a field to the road. Turn left and down the road to the main road (A65). Cross this road carefully – it gets very busy – and walk down the road opposite. Keep on this road into the centre of Kirkby Lonsdale and the Tourist Information Centre, which is on Main Street, just off the market square.

By the way, as you walked into Kirkby Lonsdale from the A65, you may have spotted two more black gates. Two more on your score? I'm afraid not. These mark, not the Thirlmere Aqueduct, but the Haweswater Aqueduct. When the demand for water in Manchester increased earlier this century, even Thirlmere could not cope. So Manchester began to look at Haweswater once again. By 1935 the dam had been finished and Haweswater flooded to become the largest reservoir in the North West. At first the water from the new reservoir was sent to Manchester down the Thirlmere Aqueduct via a connection from Haweswater at the Sprint Valley north of Kendal. After the war, though, Haweswater got its own 71 mile aqueduct direct to Heaton Park. This is the one which passes underneath Kirkby Lonsdale and this is the one marked by the black gates here. No extra points!

# DAY 7: KIRKBY LONSDALE TO KENDAL

**Route:** Kirkby Lonsdale – Badger Gate – Nook – Crooklands – Sedgewick – Kendal.

**Distance:** 14 miles.

**Map:** O.S. Landranger 1:50,000 No. 97 Kendal to Morecambe.

**Getting There:** Kirkby Lonsdale is a fairly large town and is well signposted from all directions. It lies on the crossing of the A65 from Kendal to Settle and the A683 from Lancaster to Sedbergh.

Follow either of these roads from either direction until you reach your destination. The start of the walk is from the market square in the middle of Kirkby Lonsdale. There are many buses to Kirkby Lonsdale from either Lancaster or Kendal. The most convenient train stations are also at Lancaster and Kendal. For Kendal see chapter 8.

**Accommodation:** Kendal, like Kirkby Lonsdale, is a town which provides for tourists. Not only does it have countless guest houses and hotels, it also has a youth hostel – so you have plenty of choice. There are a whole range of standards and the prices reflect this. For more information and to book somewhere contact the Tourist Information Centre:

Kendal Tourist Information Centre, Town Hall, Highgate, Cumbria, LA9 4DL. Tel. (0539) 725758

# The Walk

From Kirkby Lonsdale we leave behind the river Lune and make a bee-line for the grey town of Kendal and the Lake District. When I say 'grey town' I am referring to Kendal's colour not its character. In fact, Kendal is one of my favourite places and I am totally biased in its favour. The walk itself takes you around Hutton Roof Crags to meet

Lancaster Canal which you then follow virtually all the way to Kendal.This provides you with an easily negotiated, yet interesting route as well as making a pleasant contrast to the pastures and moors of the last few days. At the end of it there is Kendal to look forward to – a town with lots to see, loads of history, beautiful tea shops and excellent pubs (I told you I was biased!).

## Section 1. Kirkby Lonsdale to Nook Bridge

The first part of the walk involves retracing your steps from the centre of Kirkby Lonsdale to the A65 where you crossed it yesterday. Cross back again and return up the road opposite towards Low Biggins. Return along the same footpath on the right, back to High Biggins and continue along the road to return to the beginning of the footpath signposted Hutton Roof and Kilner Foot, to the left. You will be following the yellow arrows to Kilner this time. Start by crossing the field to the gap, across the track and through the metal gate.

Now go across the fields to the stone gateway you were at yesterday. Ignore the blue arrows towards Hutton Roof and instead continue straight ahead by the edge of the field, keeping the wall on your right. Cross several fields until the wall bends off to the right. Here continue straight ahead to a gate onto the road.

Cross the road and following the sign for Sealford, go through the gate into the field. Now follow the green track to the left to a metal gate underneath the power lines. After the gate go straight ahead towards a small group of oak trees in front of you until you reach a wooden gate on the left hand side of the trees. Go through this gate and follow an overgrown bridleway to a track.

As you make your way through this short stretch of overgrown bridleway you will not fail to notice the nettles. The poor nettle is often considered a pest and a nuisance but in the past it was actually grown as a crop, such was its usefulness. The nettle was brought to this island by the Romans, who suffered in our damp climate and used the nettle to cure their rheumatism. They would whip their afflicted joints with the nettles and this apparently helped the pain! Nettles have also been used, less drastically, to cure poisoning, anaemia, arthritis and dandruff. They make a good

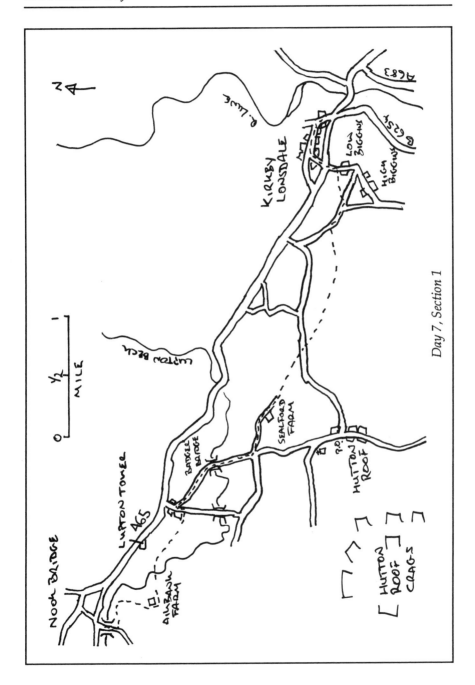

*Day 7, Section 1*

vegetable, tasting much like spinach, provide a good cup of tea
and can be used to make a delicious beer or soup. As if this wasn't
enough they can also be made into fibres from which a rough linen
can be made. Indeed, nettle was once known as 'poor-man's-flax'.

On the track turn right, through the gate, then left and walk down the
track to Sealford Farm. Follow the tarmac lane after the farmyard to the
road by the house. Turn right following the sign for Lupton, and walk
downhill for $1/2$ mile to the stone bridge. Continue for another $1/2$ mile
on the road, past Lupton Mill, to a group of houses at a sharp right bend
and a junction.

Walking along this road you have crossed the Aqueduct for the first
and last time today. Whilst we take the easy route along the canal
in order to get to Kendal in plenty of time for tea (or the pub!) the
Aqueduct winds its way through the small hills to the east. Though
only about 2 miles away from us all the way to Windermere, we
shall not cross the pipeline again until Day 9. So you can forget
about those black gates for a while.

At the bend, turn left along the road past the row of cottages. At the end
of the cottages turn right following the signpost for Nook. Walk straight
ahead to the gap in the opposite wall and hedge. Now bear slightly left
to a stile over a fence. After the stile, head straight on to a wooden gate
on the left. (The building on your right here is Lupton Tower, one of a
growing number of vegetarian guest houses.) Go through the gate and
turn right along the edge of the field to the corner and a stile.

Go over the stile and head for the old stone barn opposite. At the barn,
go through the metal gate and follow the green track on the left to the
ford and footbridge over Lupton Beck. Cross the bridge (or wade the
ford) and follow the track uphill, taking the middle track where it splits,
to the sign for Nook Bridge at the farm. Turn right to follow the sign
through the farmyard and on the path into a field. Keeping the hedge on
your right, continue to a stile then straight on heading for the corner of
the woods opposite. With the trees on your right, follow the edge of the
woods to a track which leads onto the road by Nook Bridge.

## Section 2. Nook Bridge to Sedgewick

On the road turn right, over the bridge and then left following the sign for Milnthorpe and Crooklands. Follow the road for $1/4$ mile, turning left at the junction, to the bridge over the canal. Cross the bridge then immediately left and down to the canal tow-path. Turn left on the tow-path, under the bridge and follow the canal for $3/4$ mile until you reach the M6. Here you pass under the motorway on the road then rejoin the canal on the other side. Continue by the canal for another $2^1/4$ miles to where the canal runs out of water and becomes an empty, disused canal.

*Lancaster Canal, Near Crooklands.*

Following Lancaster canal provides no navigation problems and, as along the Leeds and Liverpool canal, it gives you time to look around you. You probably won't see any boats along this stretch of the water since it ends not far from here and not many boats bother coming up the canal this far  just to turn round and go back.

You will, however, be able to spot many different wild flowers along this part of the canal.

Meadowsweet with its clusters of small, creamy flowers, is plentiful as is cranesbill, red campion, stitchwort and knapweed. Meadowsweet, along with willow bark, yielded the first salicylic acid to chemists in the 1830's. This natural pain-killer was used to produce one of the world's first drugs, Aspirin. Indeed, the name aspirin comes from the old botanical name for meadowsweet. You may

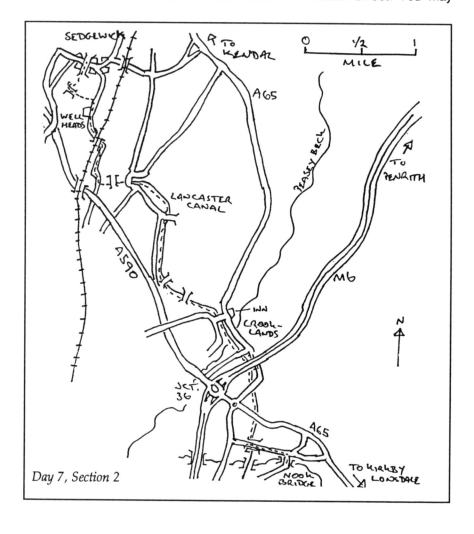

*Day 7, Section 2*

like to know that by coming off the canal tow-path at the second
bridge after the M6, you will find yourself in the small village of
Crooklands. There is a very nice inn here which serves good food
and decent beer and is a convenient spot for lunch.

Where the canal runs out of water, continue along the disused tow-path
following the sign for Kendal. Follow the route of the canal for $1/2$ mile
to the road. Here turn right and follow the road for 1 mile, passing Well
Head Farm on the way, to an iron kissing gate on the left opposite the
signpost for Stainton. Go through the gate and make your way up to the
power line pole ahead. From here bear left and downhill to the left of
the copse on the opposite side of the field. Here there is a bridge over
the empty canal. Cross the bridge and turn left back onto the tow-path.
Follow the tow-path for $1/4$ mile until you are on the high viaduct over
the small hamlet of Sedgewick.

Sedgewick, once a centre for gunpowder, is now a small hamlet of
a few houses and a post office. It also happens to be the 100 mile
point on the Thirlmere Way – only 37 miles left to go.

## Section 3. Sedgewick to Kendal

Continue to follow the old canal for 1 mile as it leads under old bridges,
now stranded in the middle of the field like a folly, through some woods
and on until it comes to a road bridge over the 'canal'.

The first section of Lancaster canal was opened in 1789 and then
extended to Kendal in 1819. The canal was built to carry coal north
to Lancaster and Kendal and wool and lime south to Manchester
and Liverpool. It was designed originally to link up with the Leeds
and Liverpool canal near Walton-le-Dale. This, however, never
happened since the crossing of the river Ribble proved too much of
a problem and the canal was left in two parts – one from Kendal to
Preston north of the Ribble and another from Johnson's Hillock to
Clayton, south of the Ribble. The two parts were joined at one time
by a tramway carried over the Ribble on a bridge. Only the
northern part of the canal exists today and is used for pleasure
craft and fishing. This stretch of canal to Kendal has long since
been emptied and disused.

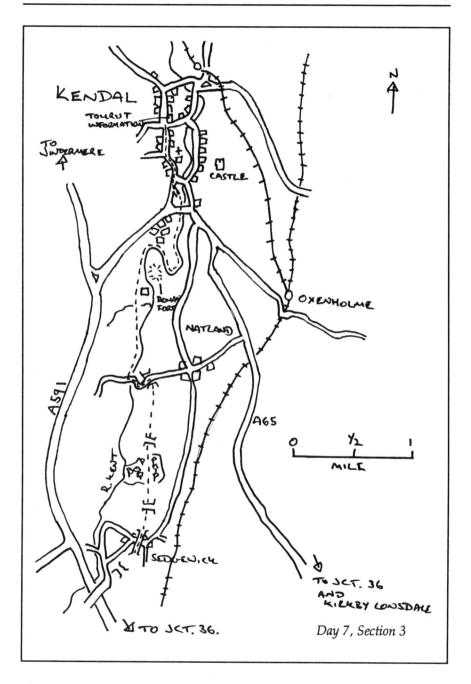

*Day 7, Section 3*

Go up onto the road at the bridge and turn left. Cross the river Kent on the road after 350 yards and then turn right through the metal gates, following the signpost for Scroggs Lane. Now follow the path by the river over several stiles to where the path splits after a narrow gap in the wall. Here take the left hand path away from the river, across the field and stream and onto the road. Cross the road to rejoin the riverside and follow the river behind the houses.

On the opposite bank of the river here lies the Roman fort of Alavana. The fort here at Kendal marked the start of the road which drove right across the middle of the Lake District to Ravenglass on the west coast. By placing small forts of around 500 men along the road, the Romans were able to keep the troublesome natives in control. (That's when they weren't whipping each other with nettles). The remains of two of these forts can still be seen at Ambleside *(Galava)* and Hardknott Pass *(Mediobog-dum)*.

Kendal has always been an important crossroads and trading post, even before the Romans. This is why there are so many inns and pubs in the town, which also suits today's travellers.

Continue by the river for nearly 1 mile as it flows past the works and on into the heart of Kendal. At the new road bridge cross the road and rejoin the riverside path for another $1/_4$ mile until it leads you onto a minor road opposite a bed and breakfast. Follow this road to the main road (Highgate). Turn right and follow this road for $1/_2$ mile to the first set of traffic lights. The Town Hall and the Tourist Information Centre are on the right.

Having found somewhere to stay the night and after a short rest from the day's walk, get out and explore Kendal. There is plenty to see. There are the yards which line the main street. These small courtyards of houses with a narrow entrance onto the main street were built in the Middle Ages. The narrow entrances could be easily blocked and defended from those rampaging Scots and were built with this in mind. Another defensive structure in Kendal is the castle. Built in the 12th century, the castle's main claim to fame is that of birthplace to Catherine Parr, the sixth and last wife of Henry VIII. It is worth making the climb up to the ruins of the castle as it commands a fine view of the town.

Another building worth visiting is the Holy Trinity church which lies at the south end of the town, just off the main street. This massive church is said to be one of the largest parish churches in the country. With 5 wide aisles and an 80 ft. tower sporting 10 bells, it might well be. Inside you will find the helmet and sword of 'Robin the Devil', a local Royalist during the Civil War. He rode his horse into the church looking for his enemy, Colonel Briggs, but was forced to leave in a hurry when the congregation turned on him in anger.

In his haste he dropped his hat and sword and for some reason never bothered to go back for them.

If historical buildings are not your cup of tea, then Kendal has many fine shops including the most delicious chocolate shop where you can get almost anything in chocolate. It even has a chocolate fountain!

*One of the small streets to explore in Kendal.*

# DAY 8: KENDAL TO WINDERMERE

**Route:** Kendal – Burnside – Cowans Head – Staveley – Windermere.

**Distance:** 10 miles

**Map:** O.S. Landranger 1:50,000 No. 97 Kendal to Morecambe or O.S. Outdoor Leisure 1:25,000 South East Lakes.

**Getting There:** Kendal, and the start of the walk, is no problem to get to by car. It lies at the junction of several A-roads including the A6 and the A65. It is clearly signposted from Junction 36 of the M6. Parking in Kendal can be a problem and the only free parking, by the river near the bus station, gets full very quickly. There are several other car parks, including the Westmorland shopping centre, but these are all pay and display.

There are many buses to Kendal from all over the area. Buses from Lancaster, Kirkby Lonsdale and Windermere are plentiful. Kendal has its own train station, the first stop on the branch line from Oxenholme to Windermere. For Windermere see chapter 9.

**Accommodation:** Windermere, again provides no problems with accommodation, there being many guest houses and hotels in the town. The Tourist Information Centre in Windermere is situated right next to the railway station and can get very busy, so it is probably wise to book somewhere in advance:

Windermere Tourist Information Centre, Victoria Street, Cumbria, LA23 1AD. Tel. (09662) 6499.

---

# The Walk

---

The next two days are both short, easy walks giving you the chance to take things easy and admire the scenery before the final assault on Thirlmere. My original plan was to complete the walk in 9 days by walking from Kendal to Ambleside one day and then Ambleside to Thirlmere the next. However, when I actually came to do the walk, I found the last day of 17$^1$/$_2$ miles hard going, especially with the climb up to Grizedale Tarn. Instead, I have divided the Lakes' section into 3 parts of 10, 9 and 13$^1$/$_2$ miles, giving you plenty of time on the final day to enjoy the achievement of finishing. If you are one of those people who takes 17$^1$/$_2$ miles in a day in their stride, then there is no reason why you can't finish the walk in 9 days. Show off!

Today's walk is then, a short stroll to Windermere. You start by following the river Kent out of Kendal to Burnside and Bowston. Here you join up with the Dalesway, a 81 mile footpath from Ilkley Bridge in Yorkshire to Bowness on Windermere. This takes you along the river to Staveley and then around the small, knobbly hills of the South Lakes to Windermere.

## Section 1. Kendal to Staveley

From where ever you are in Kendal find your way to the west bank of the river and start to follow the river upstream.

> The river Kent gave Kendal its name (Kent-Dale) and also provided the source for the many woollen mills which have been built in Kendal. Kendal's prosperity was once based on wool and the town's motto is 'Wool is my bread'. During the Middle Ages some of the largest sheep runs in Europe were to be found around Kendal and Kendal Green – a green woollen cloth – was worn and made famous by Kendal bowman. So well known was the cloth that even Shakespeare gives it a mention in Henry IV.

> Kendal has made many other famous products such as snuff, which you can still be bought in Kendal in many different 'flavours', stockings and more recently, shoes. Then of course, where would any self respecting walker be without his slab of Kendal Mint Cake!

As you come out of the town centre by the river, you will pass the back of the police station on the left and a field on the opposite bank of the river. 250 yards on from here the path comes out onto a road. Here turn right and follow the public footpath sign for Burnside Road. Walk round the right of A.T.S. Tyres and pass under the railway. Follow the path to Aikrigg Avenue and then turn left to the main road. On the main road turn right and along the road for 150 yards to the new houses on the

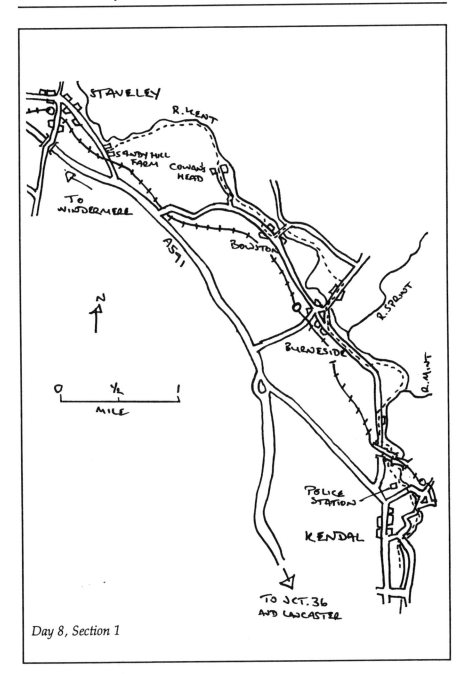

*Day 8, Section 1*

right, just before the bus stop. Here turn right and follow the path down
to the river behind the houses. Follow this path, keeping by the river as
it bends round in a large loop, then by the edge of the woods to the
main road.

As you follow this bend of the river round you will be able to see
the confluence of the river Mint with the river Kent. The banks of
the Mint are, of course, the place where the famous Mint Cake is
exclusively mined – still chipped from the stone by hand. (Believe
that and you will believe anything!)

On the road turn left so that you can cross to the pavement on the other
side. Once on the pavement, turn right and follow the road for $1/2$ mile
to where the road forks on either side of a white house called Junction
Cottage.

This piece of road passes the joining of another of the river Kent's
tributaries, the river Sprint. The Thirlmere Aqueduct crosses the
Sprint $3/4$ mile away near Oak Bank bobbin mill. It was at this point
that one of many bursts occurred on the pipeline when they were
building and testing the Aqueduct. On the 10th June 1893, the
Westmorland Gazette reported a 'serious burst' on the line here.
According to the report the water shot up 50ft, scattering earth,
stones and a $1/2$ ton piece of pipe into the air. Luckily no-one was
hurt.

Take the right fork by the river and follow this to a junction. Turn right
on the road over the river and on 300 yards, past the houses to a public
footpath sign for Bowston on the left. Turn left to follow the sign, on a
path through the field.

You have now linked up with the Dalesway. This long distance
footpath was devised by Colin Speakman and Tom Wilcock of
West Riding R.A.. It is now an officially recognised footpath taking
the walker over the Yorkshire Dales and through the Howgills
before crossing the M6 to finish in Bowness on Windermere. We
shall be following the Dalesway to the outskirts of Windermere,
before turning off into the town itself.

The path leads down to the river. Follow the river to the road at Bowston. Turn left on the road and cross the river to the main road. Turn right and after 200 yards turn right again to follow the public footpath sign for Staveley.

Bowston is home to a small ice-cream factory which you will pass on the road here. You should have plenty of time on today's short walk to visit the factory which welcomes visitors and holds open-days to show how their ice-cream is made. You might even get a free sample!

Follow the path, now on the opposite bank of the river, to another road. Turn right and follow this road past Cowan Head holiday home and then a row of white cottages, to rejoin the river path.

Passing Cowan Head, you crossed over the pipeline which takes water from Lake Windermere. When water demand increased in the 1960s, Manchester again found itself looking for extra supplies. This time they turned to the 2 popular lakes of Ullswater and Windermere. Water from Ullswater is pumped under Tarn Moor to 'top-up' Haweswater whilst water from Windermere is taken to the water authority's massive treatment works and control centre at Watchgate in the Sprint Valley.

From here the men of North West Water push a few buttons and control the flow from the four lakes and reservoirs of Thirlmere, Haweswater, Ullswater and Windermere. Because of Ullswater and Windermere's popularity and use for leisure, the amount of water taken from them is strictly controlled. Only 20 million gallons a day can be taken from Windermere, Englands largest and most popular lake. Too popular, some might say. One local landowner, in fact, got so fed up with people landing on his private lakeside beach that he dynamited it!

Follow the riverside path for $1^1/_2$ miles until it leads through Sandy Hill Farm to the main road into Staveley.

## Section 2. Staveley to Windermere

On the road turn right towards Staveley. After 100 yards turn left by Stock Bridge Farm and pass under the railway. Follow the path right, by the side of the railway. Follow the yellow arrows behind the white house (Crook House with its 'crook' walls) to the road. Turn left and follow the road over the by-pass and into the lay-by on the right. At the end of the lay-by is a wooden signpost for the Dalesway. Follow the sign and the yellow arrow along the lane. The lane becomes a path which leads through several fields and onto a lane opposite a farm. Turn right and follow the lane for one mile to a T-junction.

*Crook House, Near Windermere- Note the crooked walls!*

Just south of here is the tiny hamlet of Crook where Robin the Devil, who left his hat and sword in Kendal church, came from. The lane you are walking on is little used by traffic, only the odd farm tractor. So here and there the occasional weed manages to push its way through the tarmac and grows there quite happily. One of

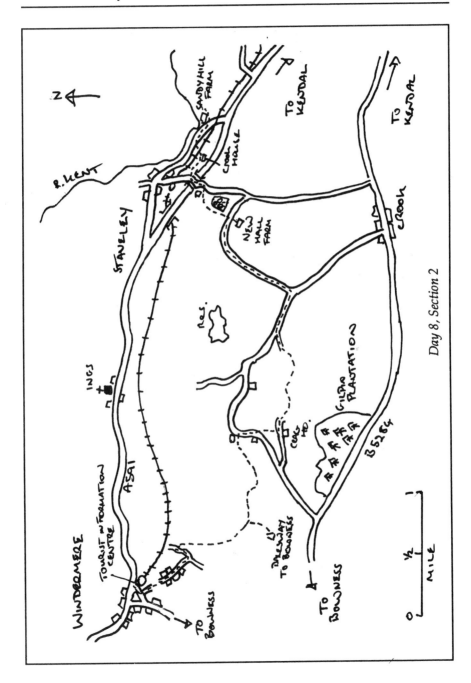

Day 8, Section 2

the most common plants to be found in old tarmac or along well trodden paths is the pineapple weed. This member of the daisy family is not actually a native of this country but comes from North America. Not only do its yellow flowers look like tiny pineapples, but if you crush one between your fingers, then it actually smells of pineapple.

At the T-junction turn right and on for $1/4$ mile, past Gilpin Farm to a public bridleway sign for the Dalesway on the left. Turn left to follow the bridleway, following the blue, then yellow arrows across several fields. Go past Crag House Farm and bear right, following the arrows to the lane opposite the old farm. Turn right, then after 250 yards turn left by the Dalesway sign. Again, follow the yellow arrows along the path. This leads past Hay End Farm and through 3 fields before bearing left and downhill to a wooden gate in the bottom corner. Go through the kissing gate here and turn left to another kissing gate. Go through this gate and follow the track until it meets another track by a Dalesway finger-post.

Here we leave the Dalesway as it heads down to Bowness and the lakeside. Instead we head for the town of Windermere itself.

Turn RIGHT and follow the track to a lane. Go straight ahead on the lane which leads behind the houses on the left.

From here you can see Windermere town down to the left. Until 1847 Windermere town or village did not exist . The only Windermere was the Lake. What happened to change this? The coming of the railway, that's what. In 1847 the railway into the Lakes ended at a small village called Birththwaite. Because this was the station for the Lake, the station was called Windermere and the town built up around it. Had the railway continued to Ambleside, as it was supposed to, Windermere would today probably still be a small village called Birththwaite. Some have greatness thrust upon them.

Continue on the lane for $1/4$ mile to a wooden public footpath sign and a little footbridge. Turn left over the bridge and into the housing estate. Turn left down Droomer Lane, then straight ahead at the 1st junction and right at the 2nd. After 400 yards turn right along Orrest Drive and follow this to the end of the road.

There is no better example of how Windermere has grown than this short walk through the housing estate. Though not the nicest part of the Lake District, it avoids walking along the busy main road.

At the end of the road go through the gap in the wall and along the road on the other side to the main road. Here turn right and follow the road uphill to the Tourist Information Centre on the corner, by the train station. Here you will find friendly staff only too willing to find you a bed for the night.

The train station at Windermere is now only a platform and ticket office.the large stone building which once held many trains has now been turned into a supermarket which stands behind the present station. Windermere station reached its heyday at the end of the last century with many Victorians coming to see the beauty of the Lakes. Even then it wasn't enough to cope with the needs of Manchester Corporation when they were building the Thirlmere Dam and Aqueduct. All the stone from Longridge, all the materials and workmen were all brought into the Lake District by train. To cope with this Manchester built an extra siding and large warehouse just for their use at Windermere in 1886. The material and men were taken from here to Thirlmere by waggon. You are going to have to walk it.

# DAY 9: WINDERMERE TO GRASMERE

**Route:** Windermere – Orrest Head – Town End – Jenkin's Crag – Ambleside Rydal – Grasmere.

**Distance:** 9 miles

**Maps:** O.S. Outdoor Leisure 1:25,000 South East Lakes OR O.S. Landranger 1:50,000 No. 97 Kendal to Morecambe and O.S. Landranger 1:50,000 No. 90 Penrith, Keswick and Ambleside.

**Getting There:** Windermere town lies on the A591, the main road through the Lake District. If you are coming by car, follow the A591 from Junction 36 of the M6 for 12 miles until you reach the road junction opposite the large Windermere Hotel. Here you will find the train station, the Tourist Information Centre and the start of the walk. By public transport is just as easy. Windermere train station is at the end of the branch line from Oxenholme and is situated next to the Tourist Information Centre. The buses for Windermere also stop at the train station and there are many buses from all over the area, including Kendal, Lancaster and Keswick. National Coaches also run to Windermere. For Grasmere see chapter 10.

**Accommodation:** Though there is plenty of accommodation available in Grasmere, it tends to be of the large, expensive hotel type. This is fine for the well-off American tourists, which seem to populate Grasmere, but not so fine for the hardly-well-off walker. There are some B+B's to be found in the village but you may find these are limited, especially in summer. If this is the case, then Ambleside is only 10 minutes away by bus and the accommodation there is plentiful and reasonably priced. There is also a large Youth Hostel at Ambleside. I have given you the addresses of both Grasmere and Ambleside Tourist Information Centres, should you need them:

Ambleside Tourist Information Centre, Old Courthouse, Church St., Cumbria, LA22 0BT. Tel. (05394) 32582.

Grasmere Tourist Information Centre, Redbank Road, Cumbria, LA22 9SW.Tel. (09665) 245.

# The Walk

You will probably meet more people on today's walk than you have met on the all other 8 days put together. This is not surprising really, since you will be walking between the 3 most popular towns of the country's most popular National Park. Having said that, I don't expect you to meet coach-loads of walkers coming towards you, just the odd two or three, whereas before you may not have seen another walker all day.

So what does the day's walk promise? Well, it promises the shortest walk of the Way and probably the most scenic. From Windermere you climb to Orrest Head for the first real view of Lake Windermere. From here you follow the hills around to Troutbeck valley and on the way pick up your long-lost friend, the Aqueduct. Having found it again, you do not want to lose it, and you stay with the Aqueduct all the way to Grasmere. This gives you the chance to contour around the hills and get some fantastic views of the mountains, fells and lakes of this area, spread out before you. I really don't think I can say anything about the scenery of the Lakes which hasn't already been said, and certainly nothing which could do it justice. The best thing is to go and see it for yourself. So come on, let's go.

## Section 1. Windermere to Town End

Start the walk from the Tourist Information Centre you finished at yesterday. From here cross the main road (A591) and turn left for 10 yards to the footpath sign for Orrest Head on the right, slightly off the road.

> The information board tells you that Orrest Head at 784 ft above sea level is just 20 minutes walk away!

Turn right to a metal public footpath signpost. Continue straight on uphill, ignoring the path to the left. Follow the tarmac path up through the woods, past the house, to a junction of paths by a stone bench. Take the right hand path by the wall on the right and continue uphill to a wire fence by a tree. Turn right along a path here to an iron kissing gate. Go through this and follow the path onto the top of Orrest Head.

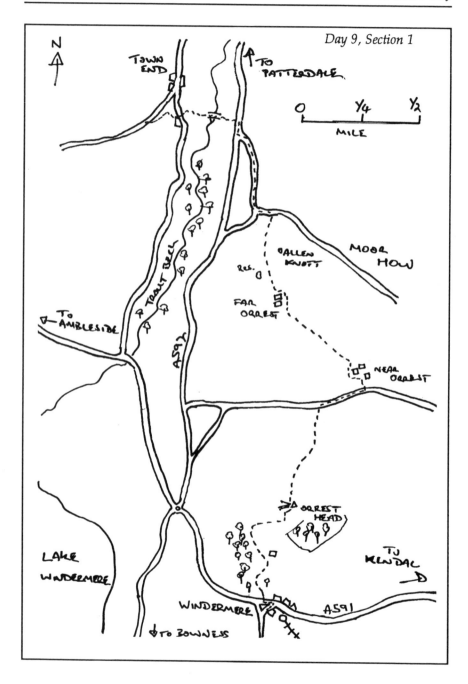

Day 9, Section 1

This rocky outcrop, above Windermere, is a popular view point and has several benches to rest on and a board which identifies the hills for you. It really is a terrific view. Lake Windermere stretches out below you with toy sized-boats ploughing up and down the lake. Behind the lake stand the mountains of the Lake District with Coniston Old Man, The Langdales, Great Gable and Scafell all visible (on a clear day). The lake itself disappears off to your left and beyond you can see Morecambe Bay and the sea. On a good day you can also see Blackpool Tower – a tiny, black matchstick on the horizon.

From the stone bench at the top, and with your back to the lake, bear left and downhill past the only bush on the top. This takes you on a path down to a stone stile. Go over the stile and follow the clear path to another stone stile onto a road. Turn right and along the road for 200 yards to Near Orrest Farm on the left. Turn left and into the farmyard.

Near Orrest Farm has a very traditional and picturesque farmyard with old stone barns complete with a long canopy, hanging baskets and barn-owl windows together with a beautiful stone farmhouse with traditional round Lakeland chimneys.

In the farmyard, turn left by the side of the barn, following the yellow arrows. Follow the arrows behind the barn and through the kissing gates to a stone stile into a field. Cross the field to another stone stile by the white painted stones. After this stile continue on the path across 3 more fields and 2 ladder stiles to a kissing gate onto a farm track at Far Orrest Farm.

What a contrast. This farm is modern and untidy with muddy tracks and old tyres and machinery all over the place. If this is progress then I'm not sure I like it.

Cross the track to another kissing gate and then turn left, behind the farm to yet another kissing gate. Go through this and turn right along a muddy track to another kissing gate and continue on the track to the road. On the road turn left and walk downhill, following the road as it bends to the right to meet the main road (A592).

We have now recrossed the Aqueduct. The first time since leaving it behind all those miles ago, near Kirkby Lonsdale. This is an appropriate meeting point with the Aqueduct since it is here that the line disappears into the last of the 3 long tunnels under the Cumbrian hills. Moor How tunnel at $1^3/_4$ miles long is the second longest of these and the most difficult to construct since it has a sharp bend in it. The tunnels were built with dynamite and air-compressed drills and it was hard and dangerous work. Many men were killed. On the 6th September 1890 the death of John Cragg was reported in the Westmorland Gazette. He was working on the Moor How tunnel near Hugil when 4 tons of rock fell on top of him. Though still alive when rescuers dug him out, he died 40 minutes later. Manchester paid a high price for their water.

Cross the road and turn right along the road for 50 yards to a wooden kissing gate. Go through the gate following the public bridleway sign and walk down to the footbridge over the river.

This is Trout Beck and Troutbeck Valley. The Aqueduct crosses the beck here about 400 yards downstream on a large iron viaduct. The Victorian engineers' original plan was to put the pipeline under Trout Beck, but after 3 years with repeated floodings when the workings were all washed away, they gave up. Instead they built a stone viaduct which again proved an enormous problem. As a result the very last piece of Aqueduct to be put in place, was here at Thickholme in the Troutbeck Valley on the 9th August 1893.

Cross the river and walk up the bridleway to the road by Town Foot House. Cross the road, following the wooden sign for Ambleside, and take the path uphill which leads to a lane.

*Town Foot House, Troutbeck.*

## Section 2. Town End to Ambleside

Turn left and follow the lane for 100 yards to a sign and walled track on the right. Turn right and follow this track uphill until it leads onto another walled track by a wooden bench. Turn left and follow this track around the hill for 600 yards until the track bends sharply to the right at a wooden 5-bar gate.

> This track is Robin Lane, the old pack-horse route from Ambleside to Troutbeck. One thing can be said for the old pack-horse men; they had magnificent views on their job, and the views across Windermere from here rival those of Orrest Head. Indeed, so good are the views that along this track you will spot a small stone pillar on the right, atop a small hill. This is one of 21 viewing stations that were essential visiting for any Victorian tourist. When tourism really began to make its mark in the Lake District towards the end of the last century, many visitors came to admire the scenery and take in the air, inspired by famous poets and writers such as Wordsworth and Harriet Martineau. To do the Lakes properly, one had to visit the 21 viewing points recommended in a well known guide book of the time. These were scattered around the Lake District and each one had a small stone pillar marking the spot one stood and admired the view from. Of course, if one really wanted to do it properly then you actually stood with your back to the view and looked at the scene with a specially framed mirror. To look directly at the view was too much for the Victorians to cope with!
>
> This interest in the Lake District, caused many guide books to be written at that time and the locals took great pride in having visitors and a new source of income. Manchester Corporation used this pride and greed when surveying the Thirlmere Valley, ready for flooding. Whilst surveying the land they found, not surprisingly, that the locals were opposed to the scheme and unwilling to provide information. So Manchester employed Henry Jenkinson the author of a well known book, 'A Guide Book to the Lake District'. He went around all the local landowners in the valley, pretending to collect information for a new book. This time the locals willingly gave the information and Manchester (sneakily) got what it needed.

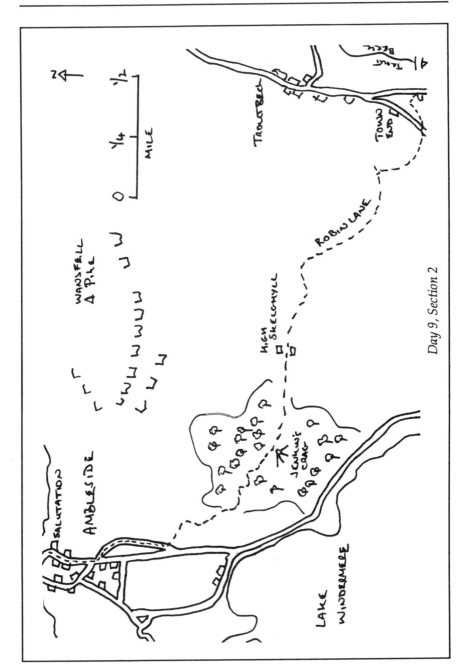

Day 9, Section 2

Go through the wooden 5-bar gate, straight ahead and follow the path which leads across a small stream and down to a kissing gate by a cattle grid and a junction of tracks. Go over the river and cattle grid and turn right up the track to High Skelghyl Farm. Walk through the farmyard and follow the track through the woods (keeping an eye out for any black gates) for nearly $1/2$ mile. Go past Jenkin's Crag (another fine view point over-looking the Lake) and then downhill. Keep right at a junction of paths until the track becomes a tarmac lane. Follow this lane downhill to the road. Turn right on the road and follow it for $1/4$ mile to the main road into Ambleside (A591). Turn right and follow the main road in to the centre of Ambleside.

## Section 3. Ambleside to Grasmere

Ambleside was once, like many other towns in the Lake District, a small market town but is now a busy mass of walkers and tourists, through which, I'm afraid you will have to manoeuvre. The town developed most rapidly during the last century when it became the focal point of the Victorian 'cocktail-belt' and many wealthy industrialists from Manchester built large houses between here and Grasmere. Ambleside does make a good stopping place for lunch with many cafes, tea-shops and pubs in which to find food.

Continue on the main road past the Salutation Hotel on the bend and on towards Grasmere as it passes various shops and the tiny Bridge House on the left.

This Bridge House, built originally as an apple store and summer house for Ambleside Hall, has also been used as a home. Mr and Mrs Rigg not only lived here, but also brought up six children in its 2 tiny rooms! Don't ever complain that your own house is too small again.

Continue on the main road for another $1/2$ mile as it leads out of Ambleside, over Scandale Beck and to a large pair of iron gates by a small lodge house on the right. Turn right here, through the gates and follow the public footpath sign along the track. Keep on this track for 1 mile as it leads through Rydal Park to a junction of tracks at Rydal Hall. Here turn right, following the footpath sign and then turn left by the shop. Follow the track behind Rydal Hall to the road at Rydal.

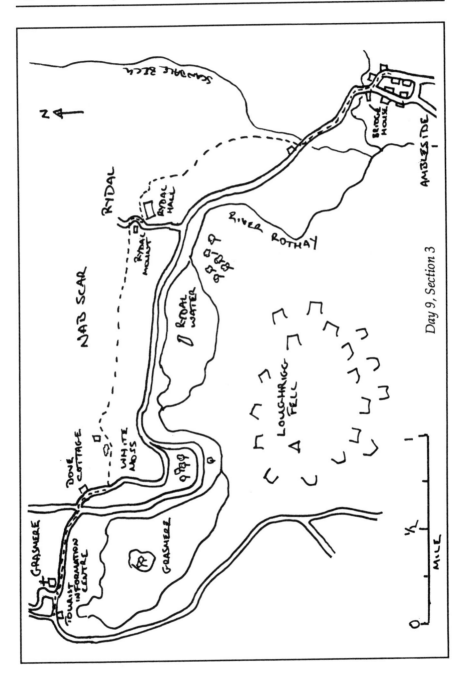

Day 9, Section 3

*Rydal Hall, Rydal.*

Rydal Hall was built for the Le Fleming family in the 18th century and now belongs to the Diocese of Carlise who use it as a retreat home. The gardens are open to the public and are worth seeing, if just for the views across to Ambleside. The grounds, which include Rydal Park, are used as a Scout and Guide camp-site and for local sheepdog trials and fell races.

On the road turn right and walk uphill past Rydal Mount, the final house of William Wordsworth, and then immediatly left to follow the signposted track which runs behind Rydal Mount. Follow this track and path as it contours around the hills, through the woods and several gates for just over 1 mile.

If you had lived in Ambleside or Rydal around 300 years ago, when you died you would have had to have been buried in Grasmere, since Ambleside had no burial or marriage rights at the time. This would have meant your poor relatives carrying your body along this old pack-horse road to Grasmere. This was quite common throughout the area and these routes became known as 'corpse-roads'. If you look carefully along this path you will see large, flat stones placed at regular intervals. These were used as resting places where the bier could be set down to give your tired relatives a well earned rest.

This corpse-road, leading around the bottom of Nab Scar, offers good views of Rydal Water and further on, Grasmere. To the right of you, under several hundred feet of mountainside, lies the 2nd of the Aqueduct tunnels. This, the shortest of the 3 tunnels at just over 1 mile, was the first to be completed in February 1889.

Eventually the path becomes a track again and leads onto a tarmac lane by a small, overgrown pond by a large house on the right. Continue on this lane past the pond to a bench at a sharp left bend.

On your left as you walk along this lane is White Moss Common. During the building of the Thirlmere Aqueduct, White Moss was the headquarters of Thomas Vernon and Company, the number one contractors on the Aqueduct. The common was covered with wooden huts and offices and a large number of the workmen lived here in temporary accommodation. Local residents were horrified about a large number of "rough and uncultivated" navvies coming in to the area, but apart from the odd drunkeness the men turned out to be well behaved, honest and hardworking. In fact, the locals did very well out of them , especially the Landlords of the Ambleside pubs. So well, that it became a problem finding storage space for the extra beer barrels.

Many of the locals also worked as navvies. The work was hard and dangerous, with men expected to work 53 hours a week. Manchester Corporation did pay well – 25 shillings  a week – though this quickly disappeared in the pubs.

Follow the lane left and downhill to a junction of lanes by another small pond. Here turn right and continue down for $1/4$ mile to Dove Cottage on the right.

*Dove Cottage, Grasmere.*

You can't miss Dove Cottage. This tiny white-painted cottage with its beautiful garden, is just how William Wordsworth left it in 1808. Though he only lived here for nine years, with his sister Dorothy, it is where he wrote his best poetry and is the home most often associated with this famous poet. If you are a Wordsworth fan it is worth buying a ticket for the house. This also includes admission to the museum next door. If you are not a fan, it is still worth walking to the small piece of ground behind the museum (no charge) and looking at the large stone beneath the tree on the right. This is the 'Rock of Names' and is an important piece in the story of Thirlmere.

If you look carefully at this stone slab you will see various initials carved into the rock. These are the initials of the famous poets who used to live in or visit the Lake District in the last Century. There is W.W. (William Wordsworth), S.T.C. (Samual Taylor Coleridge), M.H. (Mary Hutchinson) and several others. This large rock was once part of Black Cragg and was to be found in the Thirlmere

Valley. Here the poets met for a picnic and in an early piece of vandalism, carved their initials on the rock. The rock became famous and when the valley was to be flooded the Thirlmere Defence Association protested strongly against the stone being submerged. Such was the feeling for the stone that Manchester, in the end, gave permission for the whole rock to be removed. However, the rock was much too large and instead Canon Rawnsley, the founder of the National Trust, and his wife chipped off the surface of the rock with the initials still intact. These were kept until 1984 when, in a massive operation, the whole of the rock was rescued from the reservoir and the Rock of Names was restored and placed here behind the Wordsworth Museum.

There is a post-script to this story. In his book of 1894, on the building of Thirlmere, James Wilson claims that the initials were not carved by the famous poets at all but by an amateur stone cutter called John Longmire. Apparently Longmire was well known as a practical joker and was known to have carved the names of other famous people around the Lake District. Indeed, his carving of 'Robin Hood' can still be seen on the rocks around Windermere This would explain why the initials on the Rock of Names are so well carved and if true, then this Rock is a very expensive piece of ordinary stone!

From Dove Cottage, continue on the road for 100 yards to the main road (A591). Cross the main road and go down the road opposite. This leads into the village of Grasmere. At the church turn left by the garden centre and the Tourist Information Centre is on the left after 75 yards.

# DAY 10: GRASMERE TO THIRLMERE

**Route:** Grasmere – Tongue Gill – Grizedale Tarn – Raise Beck – Dunmail Raise – Wythburn – Thirlmere Dam.

**Distance:** 13$^1$/$_2$ miles.

**Maps:** O.S. Outdoor Leisure 1:25,000 South East Lakes and O.S. Outdoor Leisure 1:25,000 North East Lakes OR O.S. Landranger 1:50,000 No. 90 Penrith, Keswick and Ambleside.

**Getting There:** Grasmere lies at the heart of the Lake District. Follow the A591 either north, from Junction 36 of the M6 or south, from Keswick, until you come to the well sign-posted turning for Grasmere on the B5287. Follow this into the middle of Grasmere village and park in one of the several pay and display car parks. (You'll know you are in the right place when you hear an American accent.) Parking is very limited and expensive so it is often better to travel there by public transport. There is, however, only one regular bus which runs through Grasmere. This is the 555 from Lancaster to Keswick which also passes through Kendal, Windermere and Ambleside. This runs once an hour. There are several 'tourist buses' which also go to Grasmere in the high season.

The nearest train station is at Windermere, from where you can catch the 555. For Thirlmere, by car, you again follow the A591. If coming from the south follow this road past Grasmere and over Dunmail Raise and on for another 4$^1$/$_2$ miles to the turning for St. John's in the Vale (B5322) on the right. Keep on the main road here for another $^1$/$_2$ mile and take the next turning on the left. This leads across Thirlmere Dam.

If coming from Keswick, follow the A591 for 3 miles to where the road splits. Take the first right after the road rejoins. This is the road over Thirlmere Dam. By public transport, again you need to take the 555 bus and get off at the north end of Thirlmere. There is a bus stop (on both sides of the road) here, just by the turning for the road over the Dam.

**Getting Home:** As I have said, there are bus stops near the end of the walk at Thirlmere Dam. From here you can get the 555 bus to Windermere or Kendal from where you can catch a train to Oxenholme and the main line. From Oxenholme there are plenty of trains to Scotland, Manchester, Liverpool and beyond.

**Accommodation:** If you end your walk on this last day and decide to spend another night in the Lakes before setting off home, then you are in luck. Just about 1 mile from the end of the walk is Stybeck Farm which do a very nice Bed and Breakfast. Here you can rest your weary feet and reflect on the past 10 days before setting off home to your family and friends tomorrow.

Stybeck Farm, Thirlmere, Cumbria. Tel. (07687) 73232

# The Walk

Well here it is. The final day. The last 13$^1$/$_2$ miles before you reach the end of this 137 mile jaunt with a great feeling of achievement. You can set out today with a spring in your stride, safe in the knowledge that tomorrow it will all be over and you can lie in bed with the smug satisfaction of someone who has achieved what many others have not.

Today is also a splendid walk and a fantastic way to finish the Thirlmere Way. From Grasmere you leave the tourist traps behind and head for the hills. When planning this walk, I knew that the stretch across Dunmail Raise would cause me problems. In the end the only way across this high level pass, short of walking along the main road, was to take to the hills.

I considered heading over Helm Crag and Steel Fell and then down Wythburn Beck but this would have been hard and very muddy walking. I decided I did not want to finish the walk up to my knees in a bog and instead plotted a slightly more gentle detour to Grizedale Tarn. This gives you the chance to get right into the mountains without too much effort, before coming down by Raise Beck to Thirlmere. The walk ends with a stroll through the forestry plantations around Thirlmere before ending, finally at Thirlmere Dam.

# Section 1. Grasmere to Grizedale Tarn

From Grasmere church follow the main road into the village. Go past the Red Lion Hotel, then right, past the bank and Heaton Cooper's studio before turning left up a minor road (signed Far Easedale). Follow this road for 1/2 mile, over Goody Bridge to a road junction. Turn right following the sign for the Youth Hostel and continue along the road for 3/4 mile to another junction. Here turn right and follow the road for 150 yards to the main road (A591). Cross the main road and go up the track opposite following the wooden signpost for Helvellyn. Follow this track, past the houses on the right and on for 1/2 mile to a wooden gate before a footbridge over the beck.

> As you walk up the track you should notice a couple of things. Firstly, the plaque on the side of the house near the beginning. This states the distance along the Coast to Coast walk. Though not an officially recognised footpath, Wainwright's Coast to Coast is probably one of the most popular long distance walks in the country. Deservedly so, since it takes the walker through 3 National Parks and some of the finest countryside to be seen. I can only say I'm jealous of, but inspired by, such a walk. Who knows, the owner of this house may, one day, put up a plaque stating 'Thirlmere Way. Manchester – 125 miles, Thirlmere – 12 miles'.
>
> The second thing to notice is your last black gate. Although you cross the Aqueduct a couple more times before the end you shall not again see these familiar gates which have kept you company over the past 9 days.

Cross the footbridge then over a second smaller footbridge and follow the clear path leading up the valley by Tongue Gill. Follow this path, on the right of the gill as it leads uphill. After 1 1/2 miles you will eventually come to Grizedale Hause – marked by a large cairn between a broken wall where you overlook Grizedale Tarn.

> On the way up to the tarn you will pass a beautiful cascading waterfall. This is a good chance to stop, rest and take some photographs before continuing on up to Grizedale Tarn. Grizedale Tarn itself is a truly wonderful place, set as it is amongst the majestic hills of the Helvellyn range. On your left is Seat Sandal,

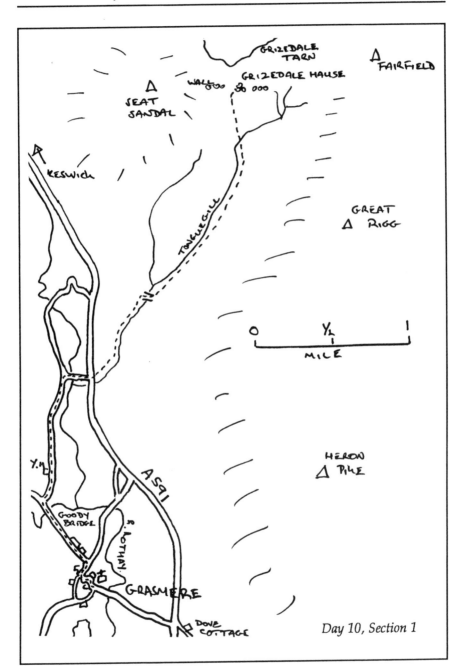

Day 10, Section 1

isolated and often neglected, people instead preferring the better known names around you. On your right is the back of Fairfield, a little used route onto the horseshoe and stretching away to your right, St. Sunday Crag, one of the best ridge walks in the Lakes. Again this fell is usually ignored by walkers making a bee-line for Helvellyn and Striding Edge. I was leading a group of walkers across St. Sunday Crag once when a young man with his girlfriend, obviously not sure of where they were, asked if this was the path for Striding Edge! He took some convincing of his real position.

Ahead of you is Dolly Waggon Pike. Easy to Spot because of the massive scar running down its side. This was once a neat zig-zag path up the side of the fell but from the sheer number of walkers making for Helvellyn, has been turned into a scree slope; a running sore.

## Section 2. Grizedale Tarn to Wythburn

From Grizedale Hause, take the path on the left which runs around the bottom of Seat Sandal. After $1/2$ mile the path reaches the depression between Seat Sandal and Dolly Waggon Pike. Here the path bends sharply right, around the tarn and there is an old stone wall off to the left. Leave the path here and turn left through the old stone wall to follow a peaty path running down the middle of the depression. The path gradually becomes clearer and begins to follow a beck on the right. This is Raise Beck. Continue to follow this path by the beck as it becomes steeper and more rocky, and leads through a narrow gorge. 1 mile from Grizedale Tarn the gorge opens out and the path and beck lead down to the road at Dunmail Raise.

On the road in front of you stands a large pile of stones in the centre of the dual-carriageway. This is the burial mound of Dunmail, the last Norse king of Cumbria. This pass through the mountains has always been an important crossing from north to south and many a battle has been fought for its control. So it was that King Dunmail came to fight Edmund of England here in 945 A.D.. Edmund won the day and Cumberland, ironically, came under Scottish rule. Dunmail was defeated and buried here and the pass has been known as Dunmail Raise ever since. Again, James Wilson, who seems to take delight in destroying Lakeland legends, points out that King Dunmail in fact died peacefully in Rome some 30 years later. Then whose burial mound is this?

Dunmail Raise is also the site of the Aqueduct's first and longest tunnel. As the water leaves Thirlmere it flows straight into the 4 mile tunnel lying several hundred feet under the pass. From here you should actually get your first proper view of Thirlmere itself, stretching away to the north.

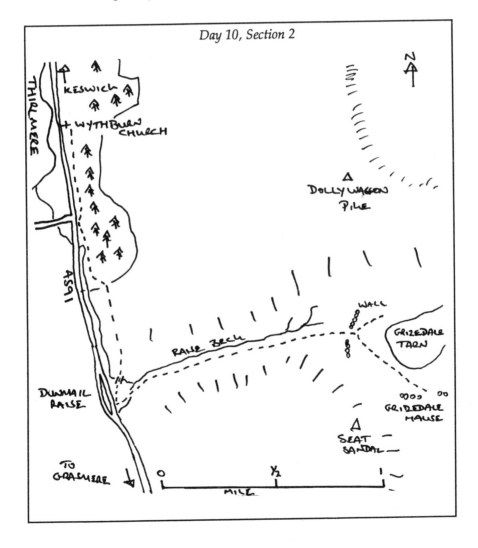

*Day 10, Section 2*

Just before you reach the road, turn right across the beck to a kissing gate and finger-post. Go through the gate, following the signpost for Thirlmere and bear right to another finger-post by a footbridge. Go over the footbridge and follow the path by the wall on the left for $1/2$ mile to the next footbridge. Cross this and onto the forest track. Here turn to the left and follow the path ahead and downhill through the trees. Follow this for $1/4$ mile until you reach the main road (A591) by a junction. Turn right just before the road through a wooden gate by another signpost. Follow this permissive path through the trees until you reach Wythburn church after $1/2$ mile.

*Wythburn Church, Thirlmere.*

Wythburn church, along with 3 houses further down the road, are all that are left of Wythburn village. The rest is submerged beneath Thirlmere. This tiny church was built in 1640, rebuilt in 1740 and, believe it or not, was enlarged in 1872. One can only imagine how small it must have been before. The building is a typical rural Lakeland church with thick stone walls and flags. The road in front of the church is the main A591 which you have been roughly following since Kendal. The original stretch of road here is now, like Wythburn, under water. When Manchester raised the height of the water they had to replace the flooded main road with a new 2 mile stretch along this side of the reservoir. In addition, they also built a new $5^1/_4$ mile road on the opposite side of the lake so that you could now drive all the way round.

## Section 3. Wythburn to Thirlmere Dam

The path runs behind the church and car park to another signpost pointing to the right for Helvellyn. Turn right and follow the sign through the kissing gate and uphill until you come to a track through the trees running from left to right. Turn left on the track through the wooden gate, following the sign for the Swirls. Continue on this track through the forestry plantation for $2^1/_4$ miles as it leads across streams and becks until it reaches a car park by the road.

You will have probably noticed by now that there are a lot of trees around Thirlmere. 2,000 acres of them to be precise. Manchester Corporation, and later the water authority, has been planting trees around the lake since 1908. The trees help prevent soil erosion on the steep slopes which, in turn, stops soil and stones from slipping into the water. The trees, mainly conifers, also provide a source of income as the timber is sold for pulp, crates and fencing – enough each year to fill 200 lorries. They are also sold as Christmas trees and you can see the familiar Norwegian spruce all over the fellside. One of the largest of these is always saved for Manchester, where it is erected in Albert Square as a reminder of the first water to be brought from Thirlmere.

Because the trees are mainly conifers, the ground is virtually bare of any flora, though you may see the occasional mushroom sprouting out of the ground. Many of these mushrooms are not only edible but delicious. However, several others are deadly and unless you know exactly what you are dealing with, it's better not to take the chance. As you continue along this stretch, more and more deciduous trees begin to appear and wood sorrel can be seen in profusion. These delicate white flowers with clover-like leaves are typical of mixed woodlands, especially on high-level,

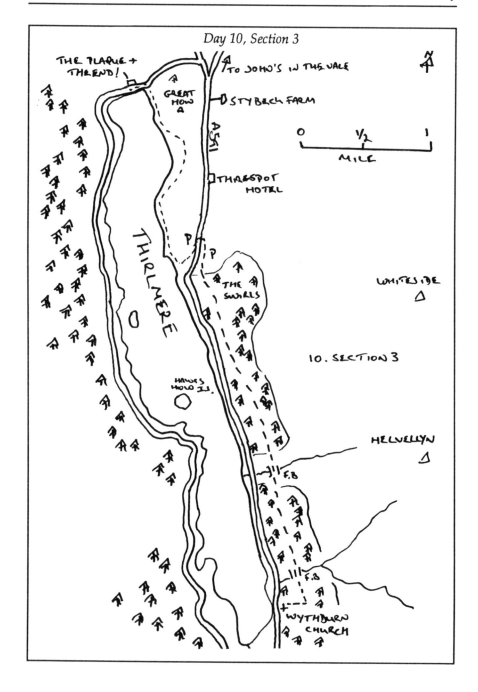

Day 10, Section 3

rocky ground. So it is no surprise to find them here. The acid-tasting leaves can be used in salads as a substitute for vinegar, but only in small amounts since they contain oxalic acid which in large quantities can be poisonous. In fact if you suffer from kidney stones, rheumatism or gout then you should not eat it at all.

At the car park, cross the drive for the car park and continue straight ahead across the field. When you reach a kissing gate on the left onto the road go through the gate and cross the road into another car park, over-looking Thirlmere. Now take the path to the left signposted Legburthwaite and Great How. Follow the path downhill and left, by the wire fence to the kissing gate. Go through the gate and follow the path as it bears right to the lakeside. Follow the path, with Thirlmere on your left, for $1/4$ mile through the trees, to a wall and junction of paths. Here turn left and follow the path down to the lake. Continue on this path for $3/4$ mile as it leads away from the water to a junction of paths in front of a steep hill.

On this side of the lake lies Clarks Leap, named after poor Clark who drowned himself because of his wife. Clark, like many men, was henpecked and decided to end it all. His wife persuaded him not to shoot or hang himself because of the suffering (and mess) they might cause. Instead she pointed out a suitable rock along the edge of Thirlmere from which her miserable husband could throw himself. This he did and both were satisfied!

Turn left at the junction of paths, which leads you back to the lakeside and around the hill of Great How for nearly $1/2$ mile to the road. Turn left on the road and walk onto Thirlmere Dam and the commemorative plaque on the right.

The end of the walk. Well done. I'm afraid you can't go and paddle in the sea as in Wainwright's Coast to Coast but you can stand on the embankment and look southwards along the length of Thirlmere knowing that you have walked 137 miles to get there. A journey which takes $2^{1}/2$ hours by car and that the water in the Aqueduct completes in 2 days has taken you 10 days. Manchester and Heaton Park now seem a long, long way from here, but you've done it. Through woods and fields, across hills and rivers and along roads and canals. You have walked in the footsteps of those Victorian engineers and in the memory of the men who toiled to bring water to Manchester. Now here you are at the source of that water, the walk completed. I hope you enjoyed it.

*Your Final Destination, Thirlmere Dam.*

From the Dam, walk back along the road the way you came, but continue to the junction with the main road. Just by the junction are two bus stops, one on the left for buses to Keswick and one on the right, across the road, for buses to Windermere and Kendal. Here you can sit and wait for the next bus home. For Stybeck Farm, turn right and follow the main road for $^1/_2$ mile. The farm is on the left here. After spending the night here and resting, you can then get a bus the next day.

Of course, you could always walk home!

# Bibliography

J. Wilson
*Thirlmere to Manchester*, Pub. George Middleton, Ambleside, 1894

J.J. Harwood
*History and Description of the Thirlmere Water Scheme,* Pub. Henry Blacklock & Co., Manchester, 1895

J. Arkin
*A Description of the Country from 30 - 40 Miles around Manchester*, Pub. David & Charles, 1795

J. Lofthouse
*Lancashire Villages*, Pub. Robert Hale & Co. 1973

Sample the delights of country pubs, and enjoy some of the finest walks with our expanding range of 'real ale' books:

**PUB WALKS IN THE PEAK DISTRICT**
**– Les Lumsdon and Martin Smith**

***MORE* PUB WALKS IN THE PEAK DISTRICT**
**– Les Lumsdon and Martin Smith**

**PUB WALKS IN LANCASHIRE – Neil Coates**

**PUB WALKS IN THE PENNINES**
**– Les Lumsdon and Colin Speakman**

**PUB WALKS IN THE LAKE DISTRICT – Neil Coates**

**PUB WALKS IN THE YORKSHIRE DALES – Clive Price**

**PUB WALKS IN THE COTSWOLDS – Laurence Main**

**HEREFORDSHIRE WALKS – REAL ALE AND CIDER**
**COUNTRY**
**– Les Lumsdon**

**PUB WALKS IN CHESHIRE – Jen Darling**

There are even more books for outdoor people in our catalogue, including:

**EAST CHESHIRE WALKS – Graham Beech**

**WEST CHESHIRE WALKS – Jen Darling**

**WEST PENNINE WALKS – Mike Cresswell**

**NEWARK AND SHERWOOD RAMBLES – Malcolm McKenzie**

**RAMBLES AROUND MANCHESTER – Mike Cresswell**

**WESTERN LAKELAND RAMBLES – Gordon Brown**

**WELSH WALKS: Dolgellau and the Cambrian Coast**
**– Laurence Main**

**OFF-BEAT CYCLING IN THE PEAK DISTRICT – Clive Smith**

**THE GREATER MANCHESTER BOUNDARY WALK –**
**Graham Phythian**

*And there's more . . .*

We also publish:

**Guidebooks for local towns**

**A guide to the pubs of 'Old Lancashire'**

**Spooky stories**

**Myths and Legends**

**Football books**

**and, under our Sigma Press banner,
over 100 computer books!**

All of our books are available from your local bookshop.

In case of difficulty, or to obtain our complete catalogue, please contact:

**Sigma Leisure,
1 South Oak Lane,
Wilmslow, Cheshire SK9 6AR**

**Phone: 0625 - 531035 Fax: 0625 - 536800**

**ACCESS and VISA orders welcome!**